REFRIGERANT USAGE CERTIFICATION

A Study Guide for Service Technicians
Second Edition

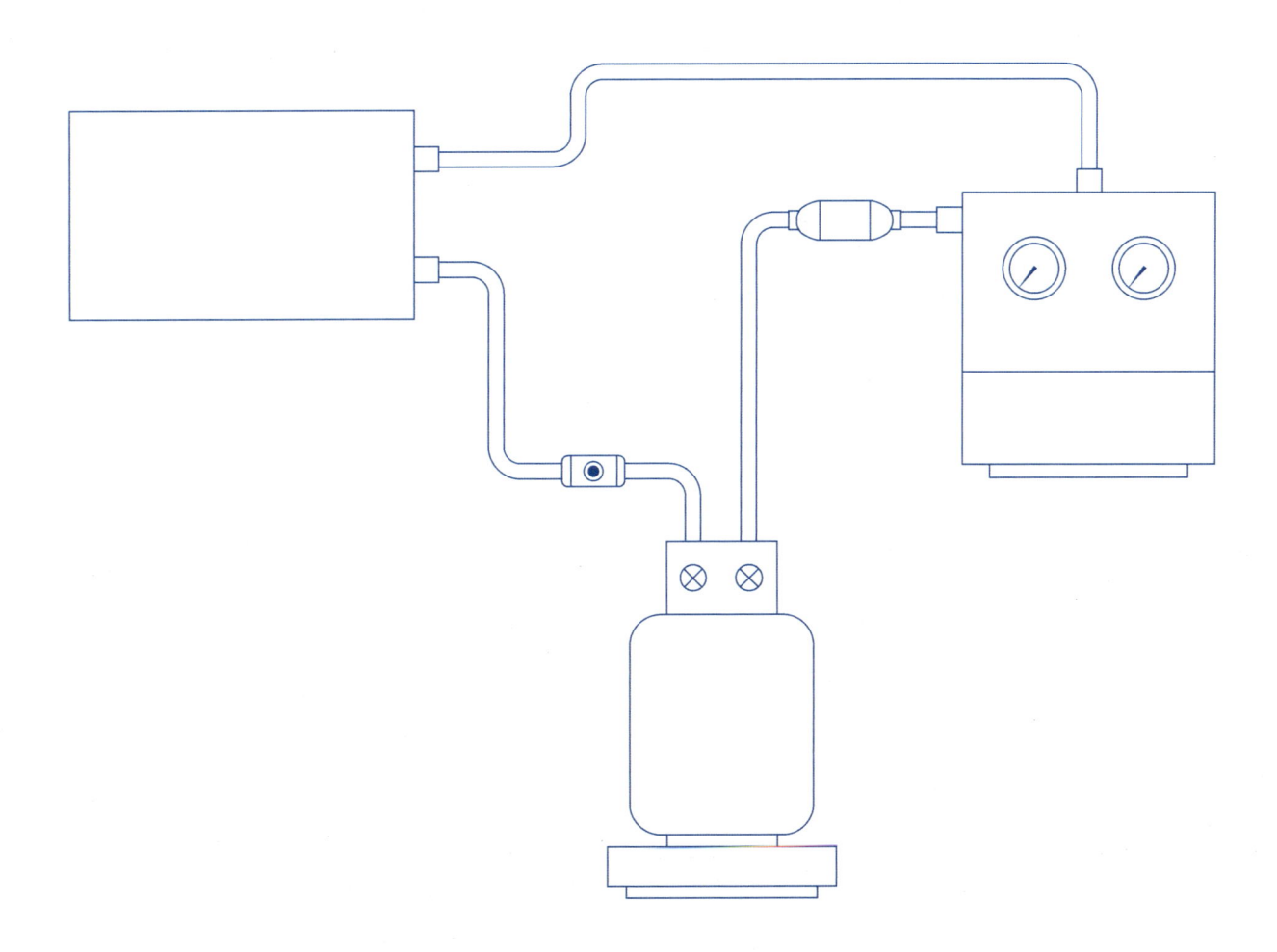

RSES
The HVACR Training Authority

THE INFORMATION CONTAINED IN THIS BOOK is intended solely for educational purposes. Procedures described are to be used only by persons who have the appropriate technical skills and the required training, at their own discretion and risk.

When procedures described in this book differ from those of a specific equipment manufacturer, the equipment manufacturer's instructions should be followed.

Technical and legislative information presented is current as of the date of original publication. Due to rapidly advancing technology and changing regulations in this field, no assurance can be made for the accuracy of this information into the future.

Neither RSES nor any of the contributing persons or organizations assumes any liability for use of the information presented in this publication.

Customary U.S. units of measure are used throughout this book. Temperatures generally are expressed in degrees Fahrenheit. If this material is being used outside U.S. jurisdictions, it is recommended that temperature-pressure tables, metric conversion charts, and other aids be procured in order to ensure accurate and appropriate units of measure.

ISBN-13: 978-1-61607-209-4
ISBN-10: 1-61607-209-1

© Copyright 2018, 2001 by the Refrigeration Service Engineers Society
First Printing

TABLE OF CONTENTS

CORE: GENERAL KNOWLEDGE

OZONE DEPLETION 11
    Stratospheric ozone
    Tropospheric ozone
    Depletion of stratospheric ozone

HEALTH AND ENVIRONMENTAL EFFECTS 14
    Human health effects
    Other impacts
    Global nature of the problem
    Evidence

EARLY CONTROLS ON CFCs 16

THE MONTREAL PROTOCOL 16

U.S. CLEAN AIR ACT AMENDMENTS 17
    Phase-out schedule
    Prohibition on venting

HARMFUL EFFECTS OF CHLORINE 22

GLOBAL WARMING 23

REFRIGERANT FAMILIES 23
    CFCs
    HCFCs
    HFCs
    HFOs
    HCs
    Natural refrigerants

REFRIGERANT BLENDS 25
    Azeotropes
    Zeotropes

REFRIGERANT OILS 26
    Mineral oils
    Alkylbenzene oils
    Polyolester oils

ASHRAE STANDARD 15 27

REFRIGERATION CYCLE 28
    The basic refrigeration system
    Refrigerants
    Service gauges
    Refrigerant temperature-pressure charts
    Service procedures

"THE THREE Rs" 33
    Definitions
    Notes regarding reclaim

OPTIONS 34
    Recover and destroy
    Recover and reuse without processing
    Recover and recycle on-site

REFRIGERANT RECOVERY METHODS 35
    Procedures
    Safety

LEAK DETECTION 39
    System pressurization
    Requirements for repair

DEHYDRATION 41

REFRIGERANT SAFETY 42
    Health hazards
    First aid
    Other hazards
    Precautions
    Safety equipment
    ASHRAE Standard 34
    HC refrigerants

REFRIGERANT CYLINDERS......................46
    Disposable cylinders
    Regulations
    Cylinder pressure
    Hazards of reuse
    Disposal
    Safety guidelines
    Recovery cylinders
    Shipping procedures

TYPE I: SMALL APPLIANCES

DEFINITIONS......................59

RECOVERY......................61
    Techniques
    Requirements

REFRIGERATION CYCLE......................63

SAFETY......................64

TYPE II: HIGH-PRESSURE SYSTEMS

EQUIPMENT CATEGORIES......................67

LEAK DETECTION......................67
    Repair requirements

VERIFICATION TESTING......................69

RECOVERY......................69
    Techniques
    Requirements

REFRIGERATION CYCLE......................72

SAFETY......................73

TYPE III: LOW-PRESSURE SYSTEMS

    LEAK DETECTION 77

    VERIFICATION TESTING 79

    RECOVERY 79
        Techniques
        Requirements

    RECHARGING TECHNIQUES 82

    REFRIGERATION CYCLE 83

    RETROFITS 84

    SAFETY 84

APPENDIX: TEMPERATURE-PRESSURE CHARTS 86–87

INTRODUCTION

On September 30, 1993, RSES was approved by the U.S. Environmental Protection Agency (EPA) to conduct technician certification testing per EPA regulations. This approval was in accordance with Section 608 of the Clean Air Act Amendments of 1990. The effective date of approval was October 15, 1993.

Examinations are constructed from an EPA-supplied bank of questions. The tests, which are closed-book exams, consist of four groups of questions. The candidate must receive a passing grade (18 correct out of 25 questions, or 70%) on each of the four question groups (Core, Type I, Type II, Type III) pertaining to the Type of certification needed.

Core: The Core group must be taken, and a passing score received, to obtain any of the Types of certification.

Type I: Type I certification pertains to the service of small appliances.

Type II: Type II certification covers high-pressure or very high-pressure system service, except small appliances.

Type III: Type III certification is for the service of low-pressure systems.

Universal: Universal certification consists of Types I, II, and III.

For your convenience, the contents of this book are laid out in the same order as the examination—that is, Core first, then Types I, II, and III respectively. Note that this book presents information and service practices needed to meet EPA requirements for containing, conserving, and reusing refrigerants, thus preventing their escape to the atmosphere. It does not teach HVACR system installation, troubleshooting, or repair. RSES has a full library of established Training Courses for that purpose, available through local Chapters and home study.

REFRIGERANT USAGE CERTIFICATION 7

In studying the topics of conservation and containment, experienced service technicians will notice that most of the procedures mentioned in this book for maintaining tight systems have been in use for years. These skills must now be applied more diligently than ever.

Technicians are advised that authorized EPA representatives may require them to demonstrate, at their place of work, the ability to recover and/or recycle refrigerant. Failure to demonstrate or properly use the equipment may result in revocation of certification.

CORE

General Knowledge

THE CORE SECTION OF THIS STUDY GUIDE is intended to help refrigeration and air conditioning technicians understand the reasons for handling refrigerants properly.

This section discusses the circumstances that led up to the passing of the Montreal Protocol and subsequent legislation known as EPA Section 608 (this is the section of the law that pertains to HVACR technicians working in the residential and commercial industry).

Because you must successfully complete the Core portion of the EPA examination in order to attain *any* certification, it is recommended that particular attention be paid to this section. *Failure to comply with the regulations contained in this section when working in the refrigeration and air conditioning field may result in large fines and/or imprisonment.*

OZONE DEPLETION

Stratospheric ozone

Ozone is a gas, slightly bluish in color and with a pungent odor. Each molecule of ozone is made up of three atoms of oxygen. The oxygen we need to breathe contains only two oxygen atoms in each molecule. Chemically, then, oxygen is O_2 and ozone is O_3. The "ozone layer" consists of ozone in the *stratosphere* (the layer of the earth's atmosphere that extends from an altitude of about 6 miles above the surface to about 25 miles above the surface). The ozone layer is formed by ultraviolet (UV) light from the sun acting on oxygen molecules. It absorbs and scatters the sun's ultraviolet waves, thus preventing harmful amounts of radiation from reaching the earth. For this reason, it is sometimes referred to as the ozone "shield."

Tropospheric ozone

Ozone is also found at times in the lower atmosphere, where we breathe it. In the *troposphere* (the layer of the earth's atmosphere closest to the surface), ozone is caused by ultraviolet radiation from the sun acting on smog and air pollutants on hot summer days. This situation should not be confused with the ozone layer in the stratosphere. Tropospheric or "ground-based" ozone is a harmful pollutant. Stratospheric ozone, by contrast, acts as a protective shield.

Depletion of stratospheric ozone

In June of 1974, Professor Sherwood Rowland and Dr. Mario Molina of the Department of Chemistry at the University of California at Irvine first proposed the theory that certain chlorine-containing compounds could pose a threat to the ozone layer above the earth. The Rowland-Molina theory said that chlorofluorocarbons (CFCs) would ultimately cause damage to the ozone layer, which protects the earth from harmful levels of ultraviolet radiation from the sun. This ultimately led to a ban on the use of CFCs as arousal propellants in 1978.

Since that time, extensive research has confirmed much of the theory, and more is being learned about the way in which ozone is destroyed in the stratosphere. What follows is a summary of our current understanding.

Refrigerants that contain chlorine (CFCs and HCFCs) are so stable that they do not dissolve in water or break down completely in the lower atmosphere, even 100 years or more after being released. Because of atmospheric phenomena, such as temperature inversions, tornadoes, etc., these heavier-than-air chemicals rise to the stratosphere. There the chlorine reacts with ozone, causing it to change back to oxygen and chlorine monoxide. Not all of the chlorine is "used up" in the chemical reaction—each free atom of chlorine goes on to cause more ozone-to-oxygen reactions.

The illustration on the next page shows how solar radiation breaks down a CFC molecule, which in turn releases chlorine atoms. With chlorine acting as a catalyst, a chain reaction occurs that results in the destruction of ozone (O_3) and the formation of diatomic oxygen (O_2). The chlorine then is available to begin the ozone destruction cycle again. It is now estimated that each free chlorine atom in the stratosphere can destroy as many as 100,000 ozone molecules. When ozone depletion occurs, more UV radiation penetrates to the earth's surface. Damage to the ozone layer is a global problem.

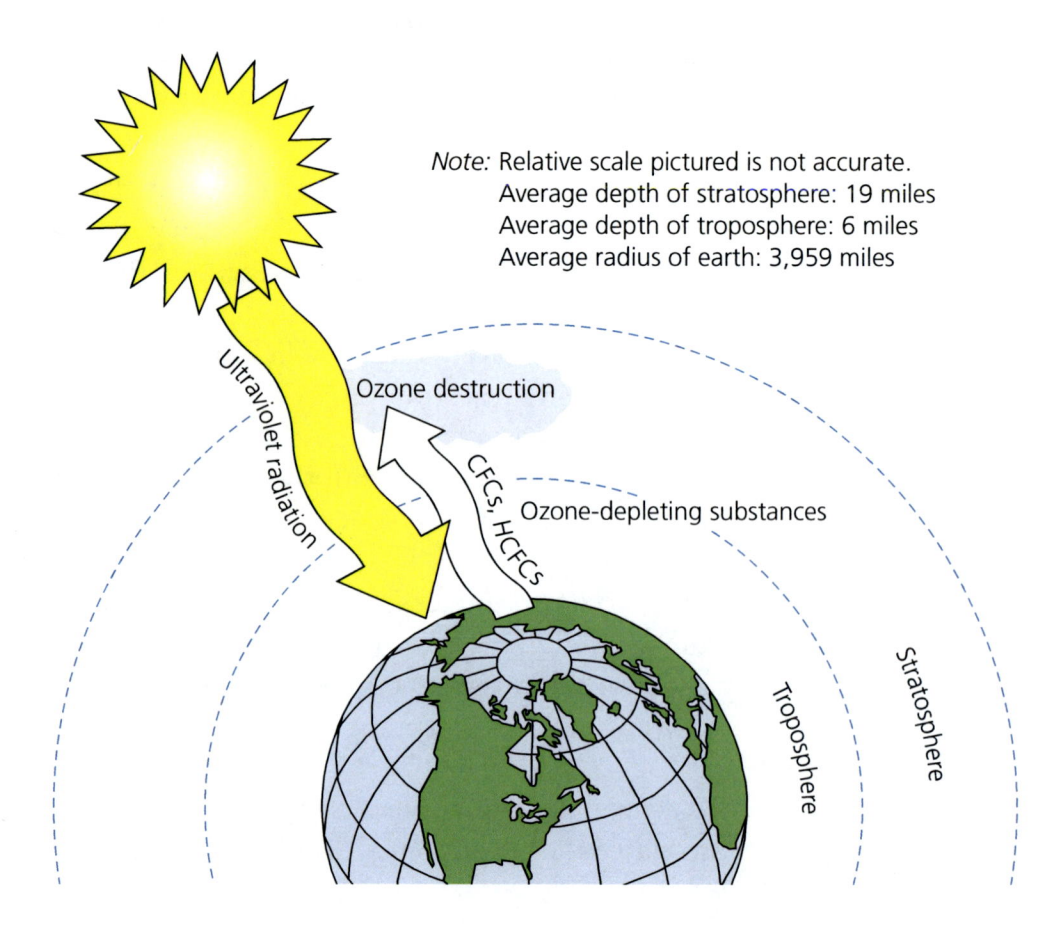

Note: Relative scale pictured is not accurate.
Average depth of stratosphere: 19 miles
Average depth of troposphere: 6 miles
Average radius of earth: 3,959 miles

Ozone destruction caused by CFCs

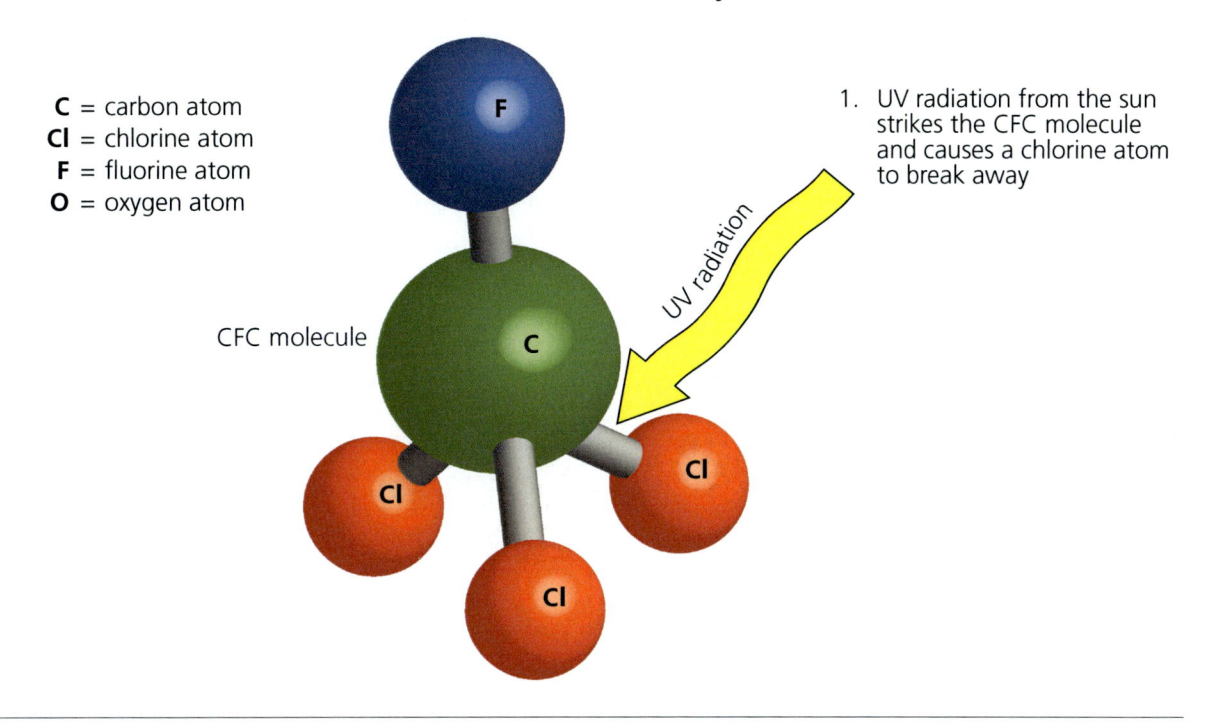

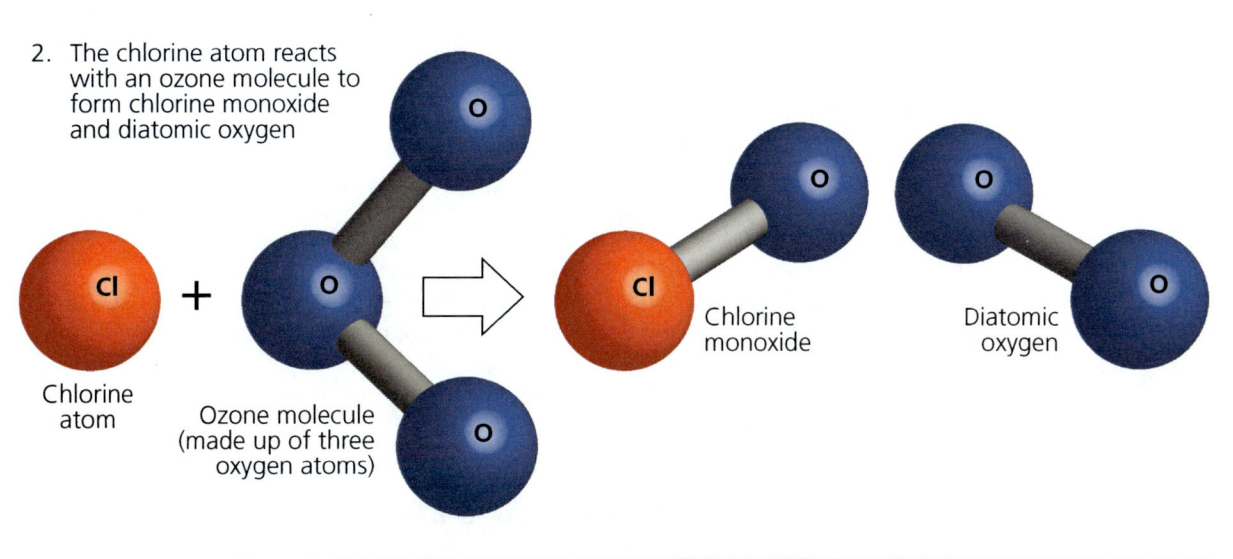

C = carbon atom
Cl = chlorine atom
F = fluorine atom
O = oxygen atom

CFC molecule

1. UV radiation from the sun strikes the CFC molecule and causes a chlorine atom to break away

2. The chlorine atom reacts with an ozone molecule to form chlorine monoxide and diatomic oxygen

Chlorine atom + Ozone molecule (made up of three oxygen atoms) → Chlorine monoxide + Diatomic oxygen

3. When a free atom of oxygen reacts with a chlorine monoxide molecule, diatomic oxygen is formed and the chlorine atom is released to destroy more ozone

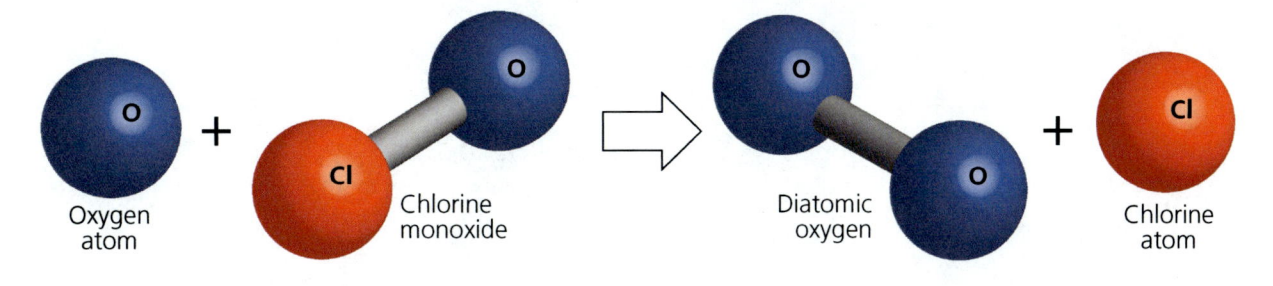

Oxygen atom + Chlorine monoxide → Diatomic oxygen + Chlorine atom

GENERAL KNOWLEDGE **13**

Each CFC refrigerant, HCFC refrigerant, and halon has been assigned a number that represents its relative ability to destroy stratospheric ozone. Called the *ozone depletion factor* or *ozone depletion potential* (ODP), it is derived from a scale on which CFC-11 has been assigned a value of 1. Some comparative ODPs are listed below. Note that the bromine-containing halons have factors many times those of the CFC refrigerants.

CFC or halon	ODP
CFC-11	1.0
CFC-12	1.0
CFC-113	0.8
CFC-114	1.0
CFC-115	0.6
Halon-1211	3.0
Halon-1301	10.0
Halon-2402	6.0

HEALTH AND ENVIRONMENTAL EFFECTS

Shielding the earth from much of the sun's radiation, the ozone layer is a critical resource safeguarding life on this planet. Should the ozone layer be depleted, more of the sun's damaging rays would penetrate to the earth's surface. Each 1% depletion would increase exposure to damaging UV radiation by 1.5 to 2%. The EPA's assessment of the risks from ozone depletion has focused on the following areas:

▶ increases in skin cancers

▶ suppression of the human immune response system

▶ increases in cataracts

▶ damage to crops

▶ damage to aquatic organisms

▶ increases in ground level ozone

▶ increased global warming.

Human health effects

Skin cancer is already a serious problem in the U.S., but would increase with further depletion of the ozone layer. Under current atmospheric conditions, the greater the distance from the equator, the more effective the ozone layer is as a shield. As a result, there is a natural experiment taking place. People who live farther north are exposed to less damaging UV radiation than those residing closer to the equator. Not surprisingly, the chances of getting skin cancer follow the same gradient. The closer to the equator, the greater the risk from UV radiation.

Other impacts

Other areas in which scientists are investigating the effects of increased UV radiation include:

- **Increase in ground-level ozone.** Stratospheric ozone depletion would increase the rate of formation of ground-level (tropospheric) ozone, a major component of what is commonly called smog.

- **Changes in climate.** CFCs, HFCs, and HCFCs are also greenhouse gases. This means that they have properties similar to those of carbon dioxide, and thus would contribute to global warming and rising sea levels.

Global nature of the problem

Unlike many other environmental issues, stratospheric ozone protection is truly a global problem. CFCs and halons have been used in many countries around the world. Given their long atmospheric lifetimes, they become widely dispersed over time. As a result, the release of these chemicals in one country could adversely affect the stratosphere above other countries—and thereby have an impact on the health and welfare of millions of people. Obviously, an international solution is critical if the ozone layer is to be protected from the damage caused by refrigerants and halons.

Evidence

The enlargement of the ozone hole over Antarctica and accurate measurements reveal that the rise in the amount of chlorine in the stratosphere matches the rise in the amount of fluorine in the stratosphere. Plankton growth in the southern regions of the world has been studied, and the decrease has been documented by biologists' research. The development of cataracts in sheep in Australia and New Zealand and in llamas in Chile verify the health effects. The need for sunscreen with a higher SPF (sun protection factor) number is frequently included in weather reports now in the U.S.

EARLY CONTROLS ON CFCs

Unfortunately, very few other countries followed the lead of the U.S. in the 1978 ban of CFCs in aerosols. Nevertheless, the EPA announced in 1980 that it was considering further restrictions on CFC production for other, non-aerosol uses, due to concern about future growth in the use of CFCs. Two regulatory approaches were proposed at that time: (1) mandatory regulations, and (2) economic incentives, including the sale of required permits.

Because concerns about ozone depletion seemed to be diminishing at the time, the EPA did not immediately pursue regulation within the U.S., but began to focus on developing "international" agreements. However, two new factors brought CFCs back into the arena of public concern in 1986. One was the connection between CFCs and the theory of global warming (the "greenhouse effect"). The other was new scientific evidence that CFCs aided in the depletion of stratospheric ozone, and that a "hole" had developed in the ozone layer over Antarctica.

THE MONTREAL PROTOCOL

On September 16, 1987, in Montreal, Canada, 24 nations and the European Economic Community (EEC) signed the Montreal Protocol. This international treaty established trade provisions and phase-out schedules for ozone-depleting substances and their alternatives. Recognizing the global nature of the problem, most of the nations that were recognized as major producers and consumers of CFCs and halons signed the agreement. Other nations, including the former Soviet Union, indicated that, following further consultations, there was a possibility of their becoming signatories.

In 1990, at a meeting in London, the U.S. and 55 other nations signed an agreement that updated and strengthened the provisions of the original Protocol. The schedule for phasing out CFCs was moved up, and a declaration of intent to phase out HCFCs was added. Further revisions were made at a meeting in Copenhagen in 1992. More than 90 nations attended the Copenhagen meeting, illustrating the growing concern among members of the international community about the ozone depletion issue.

U.S. CLEAN AIR ACT AMENDMENTS

President Bush signed the 1990 Amendments to the Clean Air Act on November 15, 1990. The amendments establish a National Recycling and Emissions Reduction Program to regulate the use and disposal of substances (including CFCs and HCFCs) that are harmful to humans and the environment.

Title VI is entitled *Stratospheric Ozone Protection*. Title VII is entitled *Provisions Relating to Enforcement*. Section 608 of Title VI contains the National Recycling and Emission Reduction Program. The objectives of this program are to reduce the use and emissions of ozone-depleting substances to the lowest achievable level, and to maximize the recapture and recycling of such substances. The amendments set new standards for the safe disposal of ozone-depleting substances and establish federally mandated certification procedures for those engaged in servicing air conditioners.

Under Section 608, all technicians who work on systems containing refrigerants must be certified. The certification allows technicians to purchase and handle refrigerants controlled by the Clean Air Act, including CFC, HCFC, HFC, and HFO refrigerants. The distributor must verify that the purchaser or the purchaser's employer is a valid 608-certified technician. The technician also must be certified to work on any part of the refrigerant circuit, including adding or removing refrigerant or replacing components. If a technician loses his or her certification card, a replacement must be requested from the certifying organization.

To accomplish some of these goals, the regulations require that new refrigeration and air conditioning appliances be equipped with a servicing aperture, process stub, or similar device to facilitate the recapture of refrigerants during service and repair of the appliance. The regulations also affect HVACR service technicians who repair or service such appliances.

Under the regulations, a technician may not "knowingly vent or otherwise knowingly release or dispose of any substance used as a refrigerant in such appliance in a manner which permits such substance to enter the environment. De minimis releases associated with good faith attempts to recapture and recycle or safely dispose of any such substance shall not be subject to prohibition set forth in the preceding sentence."

The above prohibition applies regardless of whether the release was intentional. A service technician who even "inadvertently" releases a refrigerant into the atmosphere is violating the law. Releases are considered *de minimis* (minimal) only if the required practices are followed, and if certified recovery or recycling equipment is used.

The penalties and fines for violating the above provisions can be severe. The EPA is authorized to seek various levels of legal redress against any person who violates the stated prohibitions. The agency may obtain an injunction against the offending party, prohibiting the individual from discharging refrigerants into the air. In more serious cases, a penalty of up to $44,539 *per day* may be imposed on the offender with the approval of the U.S. District Court. In addition, the agency may seek to have criminal penalties and prison terms (not exceeding 5 years) brought against any person who knowingly releases refrigerants into the atmosphere.

Criminal fines and imprisonment also may be assessed against any individual who makes any false material statement or representation in any report, notice, or application required by the EPA. In addition to being fined, the technician may lose his or her certification.

Violations of the Clean Air Act include:

▶ knowingly releasing refrigerants while repairing appliances

▶ failing to meet the required recovery levels prior to opening or disposing of appliances

▶ failing to maintain the proper records.

All HVACR service personnel should undertake to be fully trained in all currently recommended service and repair procedures and techniques applicable to appliances containing refrigerants. In addition, service providers should institute procedures to ensure that they do not permit even an inadvertent discharge of refrigerants into the atmosphere.

Disposal, as described in the pages of the Clean Air Act, means that used refrigerant must be disposed of according to EPA requirements. Some large facilities may have reclaim equipment available, but the majority of service locations will not be able to meet the AHRI 700 standards for reclaimed refrigerant. Most service technicians have little choice but to send recovered refrigerant to a reclaim facility for proper handling.

Phase-out schedule

In order to stop the damage being done to the ozone layer, the U.S. began phasing out CFC and HCFC refrigerants. As of January 1, 1996, the production of CFC refrigerants stopped. The use of HCFC refrigerants in new equipment was banned as of 2010, and production will stop in 2020. (HCFC-123 is an exception—it can be used in new equipment until 2020, and production will stop in 2030.) Although the production of many refrigerants has been or is being phased out, existing equipment already using these refrigerants can continue to be used and serviced. Servicing such systems must rely on reclaimed, recycled, or stockpiled quantities of the refrigerant in question.

With the phase-out of previously used CFC and HCFC refrigerants, the EPA has developed the Significant New Alternatives Policy (SNAP) to identify new refrigerants with lower overall risks to human health and the environment. While many refrigerants have been identified as replacements for CFC and HCFC refrigerants, the EPA does not consider any of them to be "drop-in" replacements for retrofit purposes. (*Retrofitting* means modifying an appliance to work with a different refrigerant.)

Prohibition on venting

Section 608 of the Clean Air Act prohibits individuals from knowingly venting ozone-depleting compounds used as refrigerants into the atmosphere while maintaining, servicing, repairing, or disposing of air conditioning or refrigeration equipment. Only four types of releases are permitted by law:

1. "De minimis" quantities of refrigerant released during good faith attempts to recapture and recycle or safely dispose of refrigerant.

2. Refrigerants emitted during the normal operation of air conditioning and refrigeration equipment (as opposed to during maintenance, service, etc.), such as from mechanical purging and leaks. However, the EPA requires the repair of substantial leaks, as explained in the regulations.

3. Mixtures of nitrogen and the system's design refrigerant that are used as holding charges, or as leak test gases. In these cases, the ozone-depleting compound is not considered a refrigerant. However, a technician may not avoid recovering refrigerant by adding nitrogen to a charged system. Before nitrogen is added, the system must be evacuated to the appropriate level, as stated in Table 1 of the EPA regulations (see next page). Otherwise, the CFC or HCFC vented along with the nitrogen will be considered a refrigerant. Similarly, pure CFCs or HCFCs released from equipment will be presumed to be refrigerants, and their release will be considered a violation of the prohibition on venting.

4. Small releases of refrigerant that result from purging hoses, or from connecting or disconnecting hoses to charge or service equipment will not be considered violations of the prohibition on venting. However, recovery and recycling equipment manufactured after November 15, 1993 must be equipped with low-loss fittings (see "Low-Loss Fitting" in the *Selected Definitions* section of the EPA regulations).

Section 608 of the Clean Air Act also includes "safe disposal requirements." Any appliance containing a CFC, HCFC, or HFC refrigerant that is being taken out of service for disposal will fall under these requirements. All refrigerant must be recovered from the system, to the appropriate level, prior to opening or disposing of the equipment. Cutting lines and releasing refrigerant is a clear violation of the regulations. The final person

Type of appliance	Inches of Hg vacuum (relative to standard atmospheric pressure of 29.9 in. Hg)	
	Using recovery and/or recycling equipment manufactured or imported before November 15, 1993	**Using recovery and/or recycling equipment manufactured or imported on or after November 15, 1993**
Very high-pressure appliance	0	0
High-pressure appliance, or isolated component of such appliance, with a full charge of less than 200 lb of refrigerant	0	0
High-pressure appliance, or isolated component of such appliance, with a full charge of 200 lb or more of refrigerant	4	10
Medium-pressure appliance, or isolated component of such appliance, with a full charge of less than 200 lb of refrigerant	4	10
Medium-pressure appliance, or isolated component of such appliance, with a full charge of 200 lb or more of refrigerant	4	15
Low-pressure appliance	25 mm Hg absolute	25 mm Hg absolute

Medium-pressure appliance means an appliance that uses a refrigerant with a liquid phase saturation pressure between 45 psia and 170 psia at 104°F. Examples include but are not limited to appliances using R-114, R-124, R-12, R-134a, and R-500.

High-pressure appliance means an appliance that uses a refrigerant with a liquid phase saturation pressure between 170 psia and 355 psia at 104°F. Examples include but are not limited to appliances using R-22, R-404A, R-407A, R-407C, R-410A, and R-502.

Table 1 from EPA regulations: Required levels of evacuation for appliances (except for small appliances, MVACs, and MVAC-like appliances)

in the disposal chain is ultimately responsible for ensuring that the refrigerant has been recovered. Technicians are required to maintain records of disposed appliances containing 5 to 50 lb of refrigerant for a minimum of three years. The records must include the type and quantity of refrigerant recovered each month, and the quantity and type of refrigerant sent for reclaim or disposal.

Any individual involved with the possible release of refrigerants should study and follow the various regulations established by the EPA. Technicians who have been certified under Section 608 are responsible for keeping up to date and complying with any future changes in the law. It is also important to remember that state and local agencies can establish laws that are more strict than federal regulations—technicians therefore need to become familiar with any local requirements in their area.

Note: Hydrocarbon refrigerants are exempt from the venting ban. The EPA has determined that these refrigerants do not pose a threat to the environment if released. (Exempt refrigerants can be purchased by technicians without Section 608 certification.)

HARMFUL EFFECTS OF CHLORINE

Chlorine is the chemical that does the damage to the ozone layer, and evidence has shown that CFC and HCFC refrigerants are the main source of the chlorine in the stratosphere. Chlorine monoxide (ClO) is often used as an indicator of the actual chlorine levels in the stratosphere—however, other measurements have supported the fact that the chlorine in the stratosphere does *not* come from natural sources. Measurable quantities of actual HCFCs have been found in the upper atmosphere, along with corresponding rises in chlorine and fluorine during the same time periods. The rise in chlorine levels also match the rise in the amount of refrigerant released. Chlorine levels have been detected above erupting volcanoes and evaporating salt water in the oceans, and these levels have been found to be very low. The pure chlorine given off by these sources is also water-soluble, which means that most of it gets washed out of the air by rain before it can get to the stratosphere.

GLOBAL WARMING

There are many gases that cause heat from the earth to be trapped in the atmosphere. The result is a gradual increase in the planet's overall temperature. Refrigerants are one of the types of gases that contribute to global warming. As the industry has moved away from CFC and HCFC refrigerants, the main replacements used in the U.S. have been HFCs, including R-134a, R-404A, R-407C, and R-410A. These refrigerants contain no chlorine, so they do not have the same damaging effects on the ozone as CFC and HCFC refrigerants. However, HFC refrigerants do have a very high potential for global warming.

Global warming potential (GWP) is a relative measure of the impact that a gas has on global warming, as compared to that of carbon dioxide. With carbon dioxide used as the baseline, the amount of heat trapped by a given gas is stated as a ratio to the amount of heat trapped by an equal quantity of carbon dioxide. This means that a gas with a GWP of 10 would have an impact 10 times greater than an equal quantity of carbon dioxide.

Many of the refrigerants in the HFC family have very high GWP values, with some being thousands of times greater than that of carbon dioxide. Because global warming is a serious concern, other refrigerants—like HFOs and HCs—are entering the market. HFO and HC refrigerants are not ozone-depleting and have low GWP values.

REFRIGERANT FAMILIES

CFCs *Chlorofluorocarbons* (CFCs) contain chlorine, fluorine, and carbon. CFC refrigerants are very stable chemically. This means that CFC molecules do not break down in the lower atmosphere—many of them make it to the upper stratosphere, where the ultraviolet light of the sun breaks the molecules apart, releasing the chlorine. It is the chlorine that then attacks and damages the ozone layer. Since CFCs have a high potential for damaging the ozone layer, production of these refrigerants stopped after 1995. The most common CFC refrigerants include R-12, R-113, R-115, R-500, R-502, and the low-pressure R-11.

HCFCs *Hydrochlorofluorocarbons* (HCFCs) contain hydrogen, chlorine, fluorine, and carbon. Like CFCs, HCFC refrigerants are very stable but will damage the ozone layer if they make it to the upper stratosphere. The addition of hydrogen in these molecules does allow them to break down in the lower levels of the atmosphere more quickly than CFCs—therefore, a smaller percentage of the released gas makes it to the stratosphere. This means that HCFCs have a lower GWP than CFCs. However, since they do damage the ozone layer, HCFCs were banned for use in new equipment in 2010. Production of HCFCs will end in 2020. (There is an exception for R-123. It is banned for use in new equipment as of 2020, and its production will stop in 2030.) The most common HCFC refrigerants are R-22, the low-pressure R-123, and the medium-pressure R-124.

HFCs *Hydrofluorocarbons* (HFCs) contain hydrogen, fluorine, and carbon. HFC refrigerants do not contain any chlorine, so they have an ODP of zero. Because HFCs do not damage the ozone layer, they have been widely used to replace CFC and HCFC refrigerants in new equipment. HFCs do have a very high GWP, however, which has caused the industry to look at other refrigerants. There is currently no phase-out schedule for HFCs, but proper management is important to prevent their release to the atmosphere. The most common HFC refrigerants include R-32, R-134a, R-404A, R-407C, and R-410A. The diagram below shows the molecular makeup of R-134a (CF_3CH_2F).

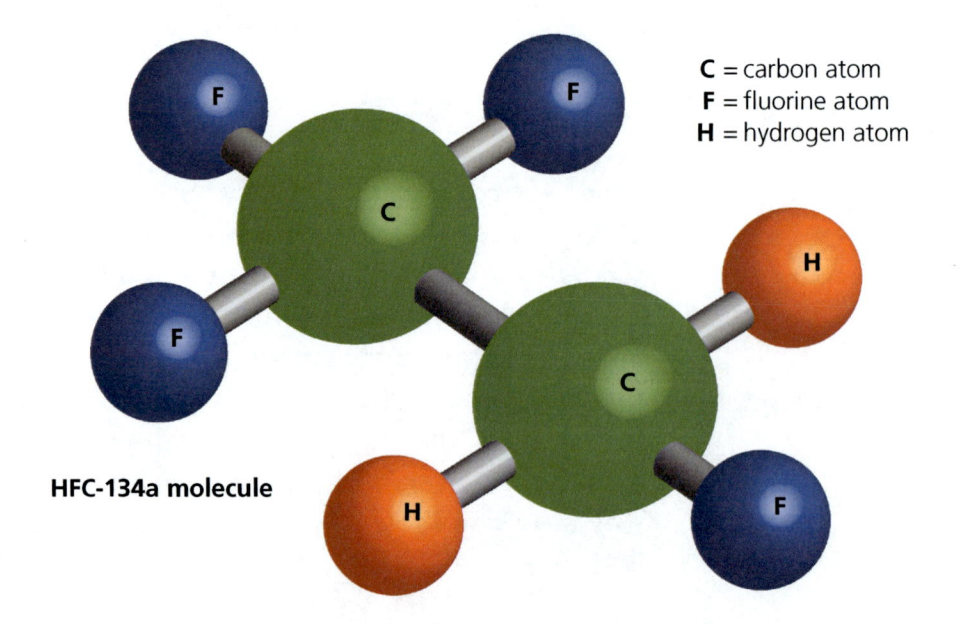

C = carbon atom
F = fluorine atom
H = hydrogen atom

HFC-134a molecule

HFOs *Hydrofluoro-Olefins* (HFOs) contain carbon, hydrogen, and fluorine. The fluorine in HFO refrigerants makes them less flammable than hydrocarbon refrigerants (most carry an A2L safety rating). HFOs are a newer family of refrigerants. They contain no ozone-depleting chemicals and have a very low GWP, which makes them a favorable alternative to earlier refrigerants. HFOs are starting to be introduced into the industry, but are not in wide use yet. R-1234yf and R-1234ze(E) are examples of HFOs. (It should be noted that HFOs are not compatible with any type of silicone sealants or gaskets.)

HCs *Hydrocarbons* (HCs) contain hydrogen and carbon. Hydrocarbons are another family of refrigerants with a very low GWP and no ozone-depleting properties. Common HC refrigerants such as, R-290 (propane), R-441A, and R-600a (isobutane) have been approved in small appliances. It is very important to remember that HC refrigerants are flammable, and consequently these systems require some different service procedures to ensure safety. HC refrigerants are *not* approved for retrofit into any existing systems. It is highly recommended that technicians seek additional training before working on HC systems.

Note: Gases such as propane that are used as fuels to heat the house or fuel the grill do not meet the same standard as gases used as refrigerants—they often contain impurities, like water, that would negatively impact a refrigeration system. It also should be noted that refrigerant gases do not contain odorants like fuels, so leaks cannot be detected by smell.

Natural refrigerants *Natural* refrigerants are those that occur naturally in the environment. They have zero ODP and very low GWP values. The most common natural refrigerants are R-717 (ammonia) and R-744 (carbon dioxide). It should be noted that R-717 is corrosive and will quickly oxidize copper tubing. A refrigerant's chemical reaction with other materials used in the refrigeration system must always be considered.

REFRIGERANT BLENDS

A *blend* is a mixture of different refrigerants that creates a new refrigerant with characteristics designed to be more desirable for a given application. Blends may be *binary*, meaning that they are made up of two components, or *ternary*, meaning that they are made up of three components.

Azeotropes *Azeotropic* refrigerants are blends that, once mixed, have characteristics closely matching a pure compound. An azeotrope has a single boiling point for a given pressure. Azeotropic refrigerants are identified with 500-series numbers, such as R-500, R-502, and R-507.

Zeotropes *Zeotropic* refrigerants are blends that do not bind together as tightly as azeotropes. A zeotrope exhibits "temperature glide"— that is, its boiling point can vary over a range of temperatures at a given pressure. The difference between the bubble point (the temperature at which boiling begins) and the dew point (the point at which boiling ends) without a change in pressure is known as the *glide*.

The different vapor pressures of the various refrigerants that make up the blend can cause a separation of the components when the mixture is undergoing a change in state. This separation is called *fractionation*. Inside the refrigeration system, the turbulence and speed of the refrigerant eliminate any issues due to fractionation, but that is not the case when the refrigerant is still in the refrigerant cylinder. *To prevent fractionation during charging, zeotropic blends should always be removed from the cylinder in the liquid state.* Zeotropic refrigerants are assigned 400-series numbers, such as R-404A and R-410A.

When calculating superheat for a system that uses a refrigerant with a 400-series number, technicians should compare the suction-line temperature to the dew point of the refrigerant (all vapor). When measuring subcooling, the liquid-line temperature should be compared to the bubble point (all liquid).

REFRIGERANT OILS

Different oils are used with different refrigerants, since not all refrigerants are compatible or miscible with a given oil. *Miscibility* is ability of the oil and refrigerant to mix together— which is necessary to ensure that oil carried out into the system along with the refrigerant will be carried back to the compressor. It is important to use good service practices to prevent the mixing of different types of oils within the system.

Mineral oils — *Mineral oil* (MO) is a natural oil derived from petroleum. Mineral oils have been used for many years with CFC and HCFC refrigerants.

Alkylbenzene oils — *Alkylbenzene* (AB) is a synthetic oil that is compatible with CFC and HCFC refrigerants. It has been used primarily in low-temperature refrigeration systems, and with some interim HCFC blends that are not compatible with mineral oils.

Polyolester oils — *Polyolester oil* (POE) is a synthetic oil that is compatible with CFC, HCFC, HFC, and HFO refrigerants. POEs are very *hygroscopic*, which means that they have a strong attraction to water and will easily absorb water from the air. POEs are also good solvents that will wash things like copper oxide from the inside of the piping. It is very important to keep the system clean and dry.

ASHRAE STANDARD 15

ASHRAE Standard 15, *Safety Code for Mechanical Refrigeration*, must be followed whenever the equipment being serviced contains 50 lb or more of refrigerant. Key elements of this standard are:

▶ The use of a refrigerant-specific detector for all regulated refrigerants. The sensor sounds an alarm and starts mechanical ventilation.

▶ The use of mechanical ventilation in the equipment room, sized according to ASHRAE Standard 15.

▶ The availability of at least one approved self-contained breathing apparatus kept in a location convenient to the equipment room, for emergency purposes.

▶ Piping that directs any release from relief valves, rupture disks, or purge units to the outdoors.

In case of a spill of *any* refrigerant, the area should be evacuated and ventilated.

REFRIGERATION CYCLE

The basic refrigeration system

The diagram on the next page illustrates a basic vapor compression refrigeration or air conditioning system. The main components shown (compressor, condenser, receiver, metering device, evaporator, and accumulator) are what make the system work, and are sufficient to illustrate the operation.

The *compressor* draws low-pressure, superheated refrigerant vapor from the evaporator and compresses it to a high-temperature, high-pressure vapor. Due to the low vapor pressure of the oil during the OFF cycle, refrigerant also can migrate to the compressor and be absorbed into the oil. A crankcase heater often is added to raise the temperature and vapor pressure of the oil to reduce the refrigerant migration.

The hot, high-pressure refrigerant vapor flows from the compressor to the *condenser*, where it gives up its heat and changes to a high-pressure liquid. Cooling of the condenser usually is accomplished by drawing outdoor air through the coil, but water-cooled and evaporative condensers also are used.

The warm, high-pressure liquid flows from the condenser to the *receiver*. When a receiver is used in a system, it serves several purposes. It functions as a type of surge tank, storing excess liquid refrigerant. The amount of refrigerant in a liquid state will vary proportionally with the system load. The receiver, if properly sized, may hold the entire refrigerant charge and can be used to isolate the refrigerant during repairs. This can decrease recovery time and speed up service procedures.

From the receiver, the warm, high-pressure liquid refrigerant flows through the liquid line to the *metering device*. The metering device, also called a *flow control device*, generally is a capillary tube, a fixed orifice, or a thermostatic expansion valve (TEV), but it also may be a hand expansion valve or a float control. In any case, its purpose is the same—to control the flow of liquid refrigerant and reduce its pressure.

Low-pressure liquid refrigerant leaves the metering device and enters the *evaporator*, where it boils into a vapor due to the reduced pressure created by the suction side of the compressor. As the refrigerant vaporizes, it absorbs heat from its surroundings. This is where the cooling effect occurs. In a comfort cooling system, a blower circulates air over the cold evaporator and delivers it to the conditioned space.

From the evaporator, the cool, low-pressure refrigerant vapor travels through the suction line into the *accumulator*, if one is used (or, if there is no accumulator, directly to the compressor).

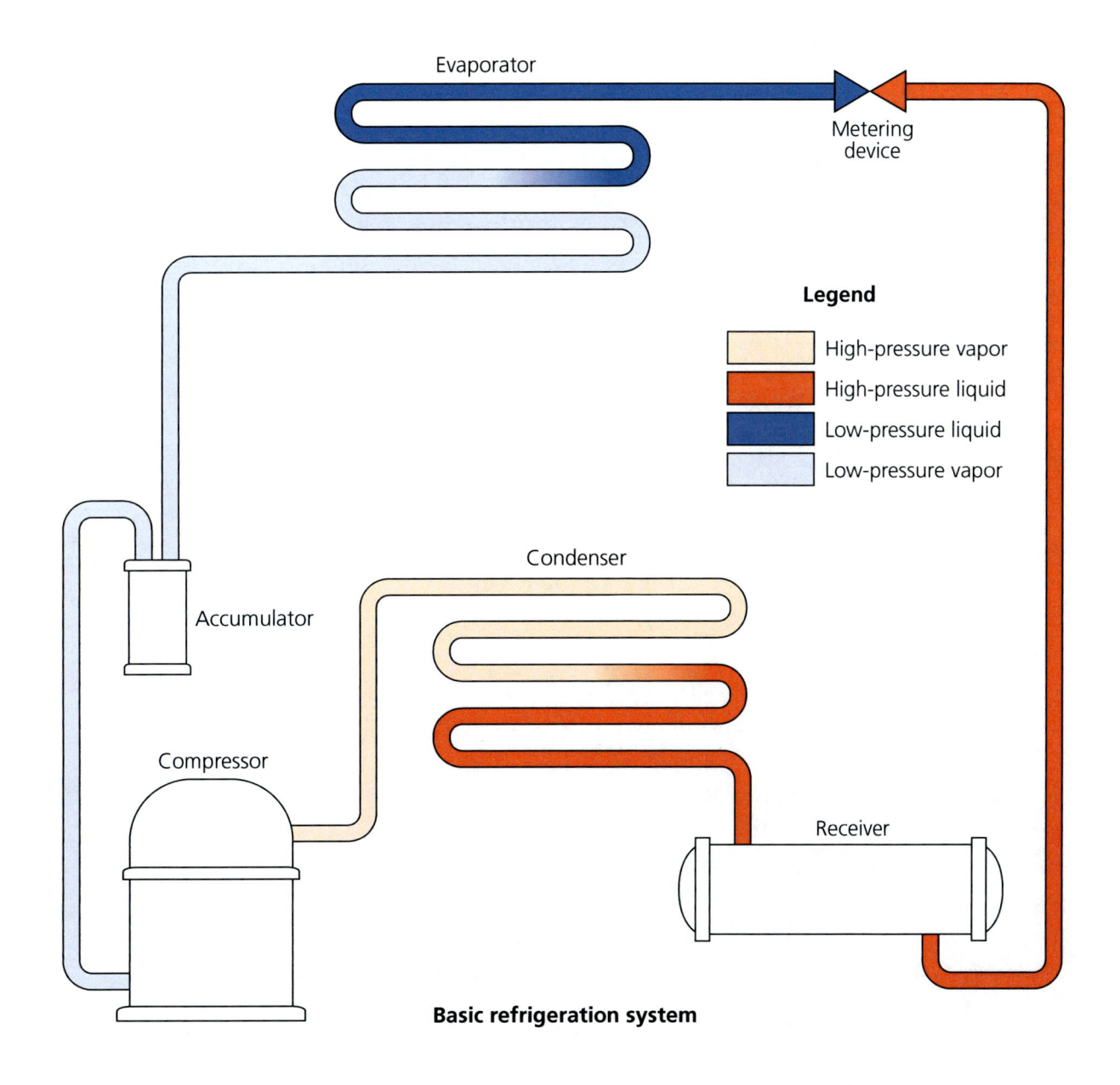

Basic refrigeration system

GENERAL KNOWLEDGE 29

A suction accumulator is employed for one purpose—to protect the compressor from liquid refrigerant. Accumulators frequently are used with freezer applications and heat pumps, and in comfort cooling systems when line lengths are excessive.

The compressor discharge line, the condenser, the receiver, and the liquid line to the metering device all contain high-pressure refrigerant and are referred to as the "high side" of the system. The outlet of the metering device, the evaporator, the suction accumulator, and all the piping to the suction side of the compressor contain low-pressure refrigerant, and thus make up the "low side."

Refrigerants

Various refrigerants are best suited to particular applications. Small appliances such as refrigerators and water coolers once used R-12, which has been replaced for the most part by R-134a. Comfort cooling systems, both split and unitary, have operated on R-22 for decades. Due to the phase-out of HCFCs, air conditioning systems have changed primarily to R-410A and other refrigerant blends. R-502, which was used extensively in medium-temperature and low-temperature applications for many years, has been replaced by a variety of different blends.

While the refrigerant used in a system generally is indicated on the unit's nameplate, it is a good idea to verify the refrigerant being used, especially since there are so many blends on the market today. Several types of field-grade refrigerant analyzers are available. If you encounter a mixture of new and retrofitted equipment on a frequent basis, such an analyzer may be a wise investment.

When refrigerant information is not available, service gauges, a thermometer, and a refrigerant temperature-pressure chart can be used to determine the refrigerant in the system. Remember that before you begin refrigerant recovery, you *must* be absolutely certain of the refrigerant that you are recovering, or you may inadvertently mix refrigerants in the recovery tank. Mixed refrigerants in most cases must be destroyed.

Service gauges

A typical gauge manifold consists of a low-pressure (compound) gauge used on the low side of the system, and a high-pressure

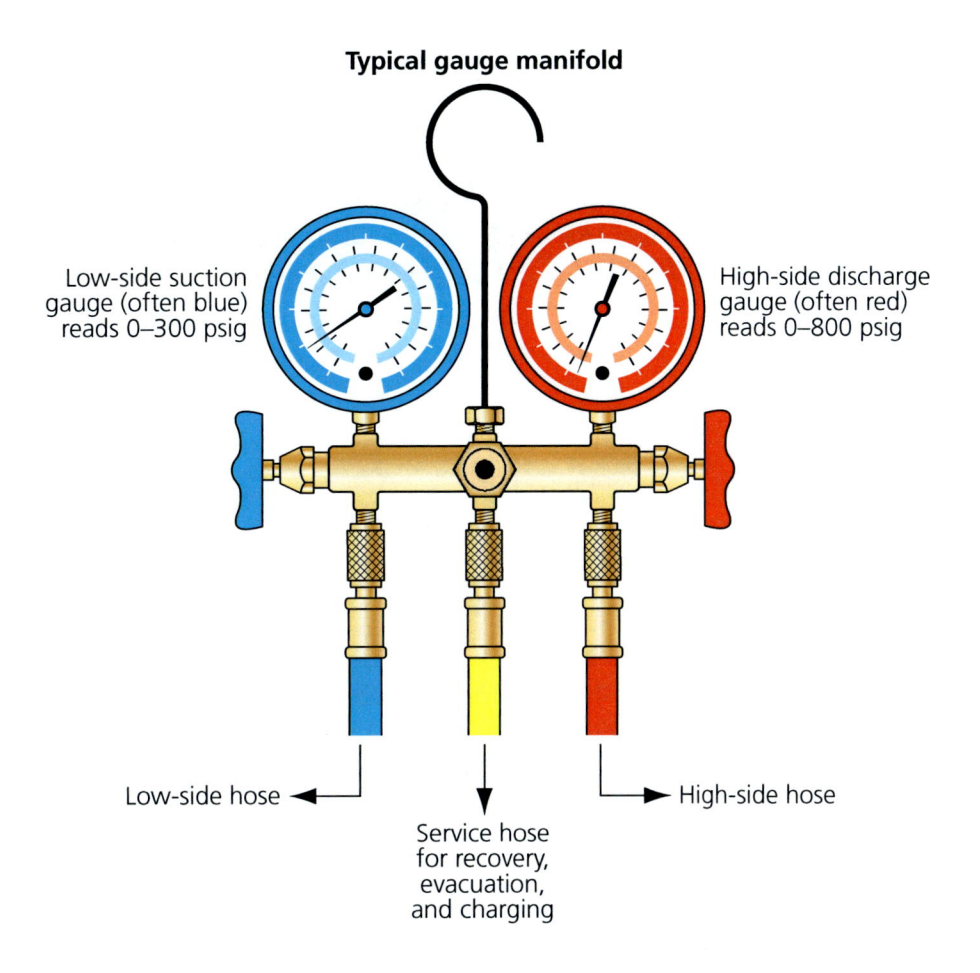

Typical gauge manifold

Low-side suction gauge (often blue) reads 0–300 psig

High-side discharge gauge (often red) reads 0–800 psig

Low-side hose

Service hose for recovery, evacuation, and charging

High-side hose

gauge for the system's high side. The compound gauge is often blue in color. It measures pressures in pounds per square inch gauge (psig) and vacuum in inches of mercury (in. Hg). The high-pressure gauge is usually red, and on newer gauges reads pressures from 0 to 800 psi. When the valves of the manifold are positioned properly, the low-pressure gauge, connected by its hose to the low side of the system, will read pressure or vacuum. The high-pressure gauge, connected by its hose to the high side of the system, will read pressure. The center hose is used for refrigerant recovery, evacuation, and charging.

Refrigerant temperature-pressure charts

In the absence of air or any other noncondensibles, the vapor pressure of a single-component refrigerant at saturation (vapor in contact with its liquid) will correspond accurately with the temperature listed on a reliable temperature-pressure (T-P) chart (see pages 86–87 at the back of this book). For example, the evaporating temperature of R-22 at 0 psig is about −40°F. The pressure of R-22 in a non-operating system at 80°F is

GENERAL KNOWLEDGE **31**

143.7 psig. R-22 at a temperature of 35°F (3°F above the freezing point of water) has a pressure of 61.5 psig.

When you take temperature or gauge readings for purposes of comparing them to a T-P chart, remember that the temperature must be stable to be known accurately. When you take a reading on a refrigerant cylinder, for example, the best way to be sure that you get accurate results is to let the cylinder stabilize at ambient temperature. This is also the first step in determining if a cylinder of refrigerant contains noncondensibles. If the pressure in a cylinder of a known refrigerant reads higher or lower than the pressure indicated on the T-P chart for the cylinder's temperature, the refrigerant may be mixed, or contaminated by noncondensibles. Conversely, if the refrigerant is not mixed or contaminated, it may be identified by finding the refrigerant on the chart that corresponds to your temperature and pressure readings. At most normal temperatures, most refrigerants have sufficiently different temperature-pressure relationships to identify them in this way.

Service procedures

Noncondensibles are not the only contaminants that can cause problems in refrigeration systems. Moisture can cause a freeze-up in the metering device and can contribute to the formation of hydrochloric and hydrofluoric acids in the system. Proper evacuation of the system prior to recharging will remove both air and water that may be present and is also a good method of leak testing. Caution must be taken to ensure that a hermetically sealed compressor is not started when the system is in a deep vacuum, since this could cause an electrical failure in the compressor motor. A sample of the refrigerant oil should be tested for acid any time the system has a leak or failure of one of the major components (such as a compressor burnout). Oil samples also should be taken if moisture, acid, sludge, or waxing problems are suspected. A positive reading will dictate the installation of filter-driers in both the liquid and suction lines. Cleaning the system by flushing with refrigerant is no longer an option. The system can be purged with nitrogen or a flushing agent to push out residual oil and other contaminants. After the system has been put back into service and run for a period of time, an additional oil sample should be taken to ensure that the residual oil in the system has not contaminated the new oil.

Preventing leaks is now more important than ever before. When servicing small appliances, always check access valves that may be field-installed for leaks. Due to the tendency of these valves to leak over time, it is a good practice to remove the solderless type of access fittings properly when service is complete.

"THE THREE Rs"

Definitions

In the past, the terms *recover, recycle,* and *reclaim* were used almost interchangeably. However, as the industry realized that more specific terminology was needed to distinguish among these three distinctly different procedures, specific definitions have been developed.

The following definitions appear in ASHRAE Guideline 3-1990 and are appearing in other standards and guidelines within the industry. It is important to understand the differences among these definitions, and to use the proper terms.

- **Recover.** To remove refrigerant in any condition from a system and store it in an external container without necessarily testing or processing it in any way.

- **Recycle.** To clean refrigerant for reuse by oil separation and single or multiple passes through devices, such as replaceable-core filter-driers, which reduce moisture, acidity, and particulate matter. The term "recycle" usually applies to procedures implemented at the field job site or at a local service shop.

- **Reclaim.** To reprocess refrigerant to new product specifications. The means used may include distillation. Chemical analysis of the refrigerant is required to determine that appropriate product specifications are met. The term "reclaim" usually implies the use of processes or procedures available only at a reprocessing or manufacturing facility.

Notes regarding reclaim

Chemical analysis is the key requirement in the definition of *reclaim.* The phrase "new product specifications" currently means AHRI Standard 700, and chemical analysis is needed to ensure that the standard is met. Regardless of the purity levels reached by a reprocessing method, the refrigerant is not *reclaimed* unless it has been chemically analyzed and meets the standard.

Because the purity standard is the determining factor, some industry experts consider recycled refrigerant to be reclaimed if the refrigerant is chemically analyzed and qualifies for purity under AHRI Standard 700.

OPTIONS

Recover and destroy In some instances, a refrigerant is so badly contaminated or mixed with other refrigerants that effective reclaiming is impossible. Once refrigerants are contaminated or mixed, they can never be used again. If two refrigerants have been mixed in a system, they should be recovered into a separate recovery tank. The only option is to destroy the refrigerants, and the only method is incineration, which is an expensive undertaking. Refrigerants are difficult to destroy not only because of their inherent stability, but also because fluorine is released during the incineration process. The destruction process must be able to contain the released fluorine. Always send refrigerant to an authorized treatment facility to be destroyed. Even waste oils containing high amounts of refrigerant can be harmful and destructive. *Never* mix more than one type of refrigerant into the same cylinder.

Recover and reuse without processing In some cases, the refrigerant in the system may still be in good condition. It can be removed while repair or maintenance is performed on the system, and then transferred back into the unit. You must handle the removal and transfer of the refrigerant in a proper manner to avoid contaminating it. This refrigerant can be returned to the unit after service, but it cannot be sold to another owner because it may not meet the AHRI 700 standard unless it has gone through the reclaim process. Transfer of the refrigerant into a storage container must be done properly. The transfer equipment must be designed for the specific type of refrigerant. The storage container must be clean and properly designed to contain the refrigerant.

Recover and recycle on-site When operation of a system indicates that the refrigerant is deficient, the refrigerant may need to be processed to remove various contaminants. This works best in small operating appliances, where the amount of refrigerant and the operating standards of the equipment allow on-site recycling of the refrigerant. Recently, standards and modes for this process have been established for mobile air conditioning systems.

REFRIGERANT RECOVERY METHODS

Recovering refrigerant is the first step in preventive maintenance or repair of equipment. Simply put, recovery means transferring the system's refrigerant into a refillable refrigerant cylinder. If the refrigerant was not contaminated by a hermetic motor burnout or other cause, it may be of adequate quality to be charged back into the system after repairs are completed. Or, the recovered refrigerant may require further processing before it can be returned to the system. This may mean on-site recycling or off-site reclaiming.

Recovery and recycling equipment manufactured *on or after November 15, 1993* must carry a label stating that the equipment has been certified by an EPA-approved testing organization to meet all EPA requirements. Equipment that was manufactured *before November 15, 1993* does not need to be certified by an EPA-approved testing organization (even if it was purchased after that date), but be sure to check that equipment manufactured before the 1993 date can achieve the required vacuums as listed in Table 1 of the EPA regulations (see page 21).

While there are many types of recovery machines, all with various options, they fall into two basic categories: self-contained and system-dependent. A *self-contained* machine has its own compressor to pump the refrigerant out of the system from which it is being recovered. Self-contained machines can be used on all sizes of appliances, and provide a faster recovery time than system-dependent equipment.

System-dependent (or *passive*) recovery systems rely primarily on pressure difference within the system being serviced. Recovery with this type of equipment requires you to start with an empty recovery tank that has been pulled into a vacuum. If the system has an operating compressor, connect the recovery tank to the high side of the system and operate the compressor to pump out the refrigerant. With an operating compressor, you must recover at least 90 % of the refrigerant charge or reach the required recovery level. If the compressor is not running, connect the recovery tank to both the high and low sides of the system. With a compressor that's not operating, you must recover at least 80% of the refrigerant charge or reach the required recovery level.

The process of recovering refrigerant is similar regardless of the equipment used. The best place to start is with proper equipment. Manifolds should be in good condition with no leaks. Hoses that are non-permeable are preferred. At the very least, they should have tight fittings. Manifolds and hoses must be able to handle the refrigerant pressures and be compatible with the type of lubricant used in the system.

Some recovery units require evacuation before each use. Many need to be evacuated when a different refrigerant is being recovered—for example, when you are servicing an R-134a system after working on an R-22 system. It is illegal to vent refrigerant from the recovery machine or the recovery cylinder. If only a storage cylinder is used, it must be evacuated to at least 500 microns.

Once the initial set-up has been completed, recovery can begin. Generally, the procedure follows these basic guidelines: A hose is connected from a service valve on the system being repaired to the inlet of the recovery system. The hose should be as short as possible to reduce pressure drop, refrigerant emissions, and recovery time. The location of the service valve depends on the type of machine. Once the refrigerant has traveled through the machine, it is transferred into the refillable storage cylinder. If the recovery unit does not separate the oil, the refrigerant is ready to send on to a reclaiming station. If the oil is separated, drain and handle it according to local legislation.

Caution: Never mix refrigerants in a recovery vessel. This may render the refrigerant impossible to reclaim.

Procedures Empty recovery cylinders must be completely evacuated before being filled. This avoids contamination of the recovered refrigerant by air, moisture, or remaining traces of other refrigerants. Evacuate to a minimum of 500 microns.

For a faster and more efficient recovery, chill the refillable cylinder and keep it cool during the procedure. This can be done by setting the cylinder in a bucket of ice. There are also dry chemicals on the market that can be mixed with water to create low temperatures. The mixture is then poured into the bucket in which the cylinder is immersed during the transfer process. The lower temperature of the cylinder reduces the pressure of the refrigerant inside it. Conversely, if the system from which you are removing refrigerant is at a low ambient temperature, the recovery process will be slower. The system can be warmed with heat lamps or defrost heaters. Remove the cores from Schrader valves, and use hoses that are as large in diameter and as short in length as possible to reduce restrictions and reduce pressure drop.

Before beginning recovery, check the positions of all service valves and the oil level of the recovery unit. Recover the

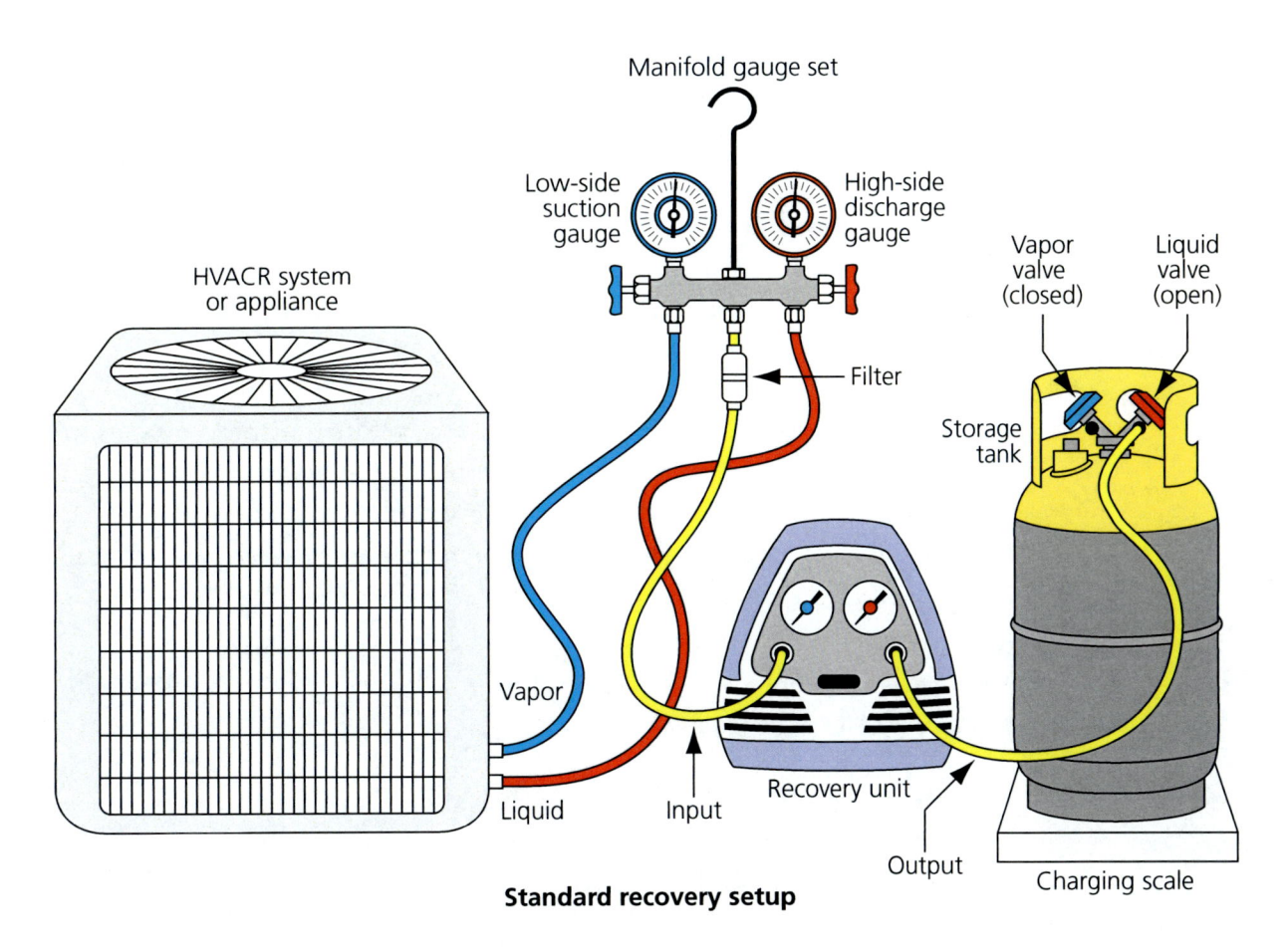

Standard recovery setup

refrigerant into the system's own receiver or storage tank if it has one. It is most efficient to recover liquid first (from the system's liquid line), then vapor. Recovering refrigerant in vapor phase will leave the oil in the system, minimizing oil loss.

When recovering from small appliances, first identify the refrigerant that you are about to recover. Older refrigerators, particularly those built before 1950, may contain non–fluorocarbon refrigerants, which must *not* be recovered with current recovery equipment. The same is true of many recreational vehicle appliances, both old and new. When access fittings need to be installed, they should be checked for leaks. Follow these guidelines when using system-dependent (passive) recovery equipment:

▶ If the appliance compressor does not run, warm the compressor oil and tap the compressor. This will help release refrigerant trapped in the oil.

▶ If the appliance compressor does not run, recover refrigerant from both the high and low sides of the system for a complete recovery. This will also speed the recovery process.

▶ If the appliance compressor is operable, run it and recover the refrigerant from the high side.

When recovering refrigerant from chillers, maintain water circulation in order to prevent freezing.

Slight amounts of refrigerant may escape during these procedures, but U.S. Federal regulations state that "*de minimis* (minimal) releases associated with good faith attempts to recapture and recycle or safely dispose of any such substance (refrigerant) shall not be subject to the prohibition" (against venting).

Safety The following safety rules must be followed when you use any recovery equipment:

▶ Use only cylinders certified by the Department of Transportation (DOT) as being refillable. All cylinders must be recertified every five years.

- Use only fully evacuated and clean cylinders.

- *Never* fill a cylinder over 80%. (The maximum temperature for the 80% fill level is 70°F. If there is any chance that the cylinder will be exposed to temperatures over 130°F, fill only to 60%.) This allows for expansion of the refrigerant when the cylinder warms up. Failure to leave adequate expansion space can cause the cylinder to explode, resulting in severe injury or death. Depending on the recovery equipment and cylinders used, there are several ways to determine the 80% fill level. You can calculate it by weight, using an accurate scale. You also may use a mechanical float device in the cylinder, or an electronic shutoff device.

- Be careful not to trap liquid refrigerant between service valves.

- *Never* mix different refrigerants.

- Plainly mark the type of refrigerant in refillable cylinders. Use each cylinder only for the type of refrigerant for which it is marked.

- Restore a contaminated refrigerant to useful purity by recycling or reclaiming or destroy it properly.

- Handle cylinders with care. Do not drop or bump. Keep cylinders in a vertical position. Secure them to prevent them from tipping over. *Never* heat a cylinder with a torch or open flame.

LEAK DETECTION

Finding and repairing leaks in a system while servicing equipment conserves the refrigerant. Using an electronic or ultrasonic leak detector is the best way to find the general area of a leak, while using a soap bubble solution is often the best method of pinpointing the exact location of a leak. Electronic leak detectors are effective at sensing leaks of most common refrigerants. Ultrasonic leak detectors are sensitive to the *sound* of a leak and will work with any gas, including nitrogen.

Oil additives also have been developed for leak testing. Leaks are located by inspecting the unit with an ultraviolet (black) light and observing a fluorescent glow at the leak. This method is very effective on large equipment.

System pressurization

Checking for leaks before recovery (while the system is pressurized) is preferred, since it makes the leaks easier to detect. In low-pressure systems, or in any system that has lost substantial charge, it may be necessary to raise the system pressure before leak testing. This is almost always required when the leak is thought to be on the low side of a low-pressure system. Because such a system operates at a pressure below atmospheric, leaks are inward, not outward from the system.

For low-pressure systems, the preferred method of leak testing is to raise the low-side pressure by carefully raising the temperature—for example, by using controlled-temperature warm water. Several chiller manufacturers offer packaged hot-water generators. Warm tap water also may be used, if available. The first step in warm-water pressurization is to valve off the condenser and evaporator water circuits. The next step is to circulate the warm water into the evaporator bundle. This causes the refrigerant pressure to rise. The same result can be achieved with heat blankets, such as those used in the PREVAC system. Never raise the pressure in a low-pressure chiller above 10 psig, because the rupture disks will open at 15 psig.

A system that does not have refrigerant in it should be pressurized with nitrogen. (Nitrogen causes no damage to the environment.) A standing leak test then can be performed to ensure that the system is holding pressure. The system also can be checked with an ultrasonic leak detector or with soap bubbles while under the nitrogen pressure. Always use a pressure regulator on the nitrogen cylinder, and a pressure relief valve downstream from the regulator. Never exceed the system's low-side test pressure.

If leaks cannot be found with nitrogen alone, a trace amount of the system's design refrigerant can be mixed with the nitrogen and then pressurized to allow the use of an electronic leak detector. This mixture cannot be separated and does not need to be recovered.

The final check for leaks is called the *standing vacuum test*, in which the system is evacuated, and a deep vacuum is pulled on the system. An increase in pressure indicates a potential leak.

Requirements for repair

The EPA requires all industrial process systems containing more than 50 lb of refrigerant to be repaired if the leak rate exceeds 30% (effective 2019) of the total charge per year. All commercial refrigeration systems containing more than 50 lb of refrigerant must be repaired if the leak rate exceeds 20% (effective 2019) of the total charge per year. All comfort cooling systems containing more than 50 lb of refrigerant must be repaired if the leak rate exceeds 10% (effective 2019) of the total charge per year. Leaks exceeding allowable rates, with few exceptions, must be repaired within 30 days unless the machine is retired or mothballed. The 30-day period can be extended if government regulations make repairs impossible, if the area is subject to radiological contamination, or if the parts needed to make the repair are not available. Leak rates need to be calculated any time refrigerant is added when a repair has not been made. The equipment nameplate or manufacturer's specification should be referenced to determine the full system charge.

DEHYDRATION

Filter-driers are used to control the circulation of moisture in a system. However, they are not designed to remove large amounts of moisture, which may enter a system during installation of the equipment, a major repair, or when the system is open for some other reason. A deep vacuum is necessary for removing noncondensibles and moisture. To properly dehydrate a system before recharging, a good vacuum pump and vacuum gauge (micron gauge) are required. A final vacuum of 500 microns or less should be reached to ensure proper dehydration of the system. For the best accuracy, the micron gauge should be connected to the system as far from the pump as possible. The pump should be stopped, then isolated from the system, and the system allowed some time to equalize before a final reading is taken. A rise in pressure that levels out may indicate that moisture is still present. If the pressure continues to rise, the system may have a leak. Moisture remaining in an operating system can cause acid to form. A deep vacuum will remove only gases and water vapor, not oil or acids. A system cannot be over-evacuated.

The speed of the evacuation process will be affected by various factors, including the size of the system being evacuated, the size of the vacuum pump, the temperature of the system, the amount of moisture in the system, and restrictions that may be present in the recovery path. The system can be warmed (especially in lower ambient conditions) to help moisture change to vapor. Several things can be done to reduce restrictions in the recovery path, including:

- Keep hoses as short as possible.
- Use hoses with a large diameter.
- Remove the cores from Schrader valves.
- Use multiple hoses.

REFRIGERANT SAFETY

The following are general safety considerations concerning refrigerants. Before using or handling any refrigerant, personnel should be familiar with safety concerns for the specific product. This is particularly important for some of the newer replacement refrigerants, including hydrocarbons. Specific product safety information is available from the manufacturer.

Health hazards Although the toxicity of fluorocarbon refrigerants is low, the possibility of injury or death exists in unusual situations, or if they are deliberately misused. The vapors are several times heavier than air. Good ventilation must be provided in areas where high concentrations of the heavy vapors might accumulate and exclude oxygen.

Inhalation of concentrated refrigerant vapor is dangerous and can be fatal. Exposure to levels of fluorocarbons above recommended exposure levels can result in loss of concentration and drowsiness. There have been reported cases of fatal cardiac arrhythmia in humans accidentally exposed to high levels. Skin or eye contact can result in irritation and frostbite. (Note that exposure levels for some of the newer replacement refrigerants are much lower than for those with which you may be familiar.)

First aid In cases of inhalation, remove the victim to fresh air. If the victim is not breathing, administer artificial respiration. If breathing is difficult, give oxygen. Avoid stimulants. Do *not* give adrenaline (epinephrine)—it can have potentially detrimental effects on the heart. Call a physician.

In cases of eye contact, flush eyes promptly with plenty of water for at least 15 minutes. Call a physician. Flush exposed skin with water (not hot) or use other means to warm skin slowly.

Other hazards Most halogenated compounds decompose at high temperatures (such as those associated with gas flames or electric heaters). The chemicals that result under these circumstances always include hydrofluoric acid. If the compound contains chlorine, hydrochloric acid also will be formed and, if a source of water (or oxygen) is present, a smaller amount of phosgene. Fortunately, the halogen acids have a very sharp, stinging effect on the nose and can be detected by odor at concentrations below their toxic level. These acids serve as warning agents that decomposition has occurred. If they are detected, the area should be evacuated until the air has been cleared of decomposition products.

Precautions Observe the following guidelines when working with or around refrigerants:

- Always read the product label and the product Safety Data Sheet (SDS).

- Always use with adequate ventilation. Most fatal accidents involving refrigerants are due to oxygen deprivation.

- Never expose refrigerants to flames, sparks, or hot surfaces.

- Never trap liquid refrigerant between valves (in the system or in service hoses) where there is no pressure relief device. A dirty or corroded pressure relief device must be replaced.

▶ Use an alcohol spray to clean refrigerant sight glasses that have become coated with ice.

▶ When leak testing a system, use nitrogen for increasing the pressure after the refrigerant is recovered. Use a pressure regulator on the nitrogen cylinder with a relief valve located downstream to ensure a safe pressure in the system. The low-side test pressure value listed on the data plate should be used as the maximum pressure applied to the system for leak testing.

▶ Never use oxygen or compressed air for pressurization—compressor oil or some refrigerants may explode when under pressure.

▶ Physicians: Do not use epinephrine to treat overexposure.

Safety equipment

Personnel handling refrigerants should wear side-shield safety glasses, impervious (preferably butyl-lined) gloves, and other protective equipment or clothing as required by the employer or the situation. Follow all safety requirements provided on the SDS sheet and by the manufacturer of the equipment being serviced.

Auxiliary breathing apparatus should be readily accessible in storage, handling, and production areas in case an abnormally high concentration of refrigerant vapor should develop. Showers and eyewash fountains of the deluge type should be readily accessible in case of contact with the skin or eyes.

ASHRAE Standard 34

ASHRAE has developed a safety classification matrix for refrigerants based on toxicity and flammability ratings. *Toxicity* ratings are based on a TLV/TWA index. "TLV" stands for *threshold limit value* (exposure of 8 to 12 hr per day, 5 days a week, for 40 years), and "TWA" stands for *time-weighted average* (average exposure expressed in hours per day). Refrigerants are assigned to one of two classes, depending on the allowable exposure:

▶ Class A: TLV/TWA of 400 ppm or greater

▶ Class B: TLV/TWA of 399 ppm or less

	Lower toxicity	Higher toxicity
Higher flammability	A3	B3
Lower flammability	A2 / A2L*	B2 / B2L*
No flame	A1	B1

*A2L and B2L are lower-flammability refrigerants with a minimum burning velocity of ≤10 cm/sec

Safety matrix

Flammability also is rated:

▶ Class 1: *no* flame propagation

▶ Class 2: *lower* flammability

▶ Class 2L: subclassification of Class 2 refrigerants that burn very slowly

▶ Class 3: *high* flammability

Refrigerants then can be classified according to a matrix, as shown above. As you can see, an "A1" rating denotes the safest refrigerants to handle, and "B3" the most dangerous.

HC refrigerants   Hydrocarbon (HC) refrigerants are now being used in small appliances and commercial cases. HC refrigerants are flammable and require special handling. Technicians should have additional training related to HC refrigerants prior to working on these systems. Household refrigerators that use HC refrigerants will have red safety markings:

▶ on or near the evaporator or exposed refrigerant tubing

▶ near the machine compartment

GENERAL KNOWLEDGE   **45**

▶ on the exterior of the refrigerator

▶ at least 1 in. in each direction from any service connection.

R-600a (isobutane), R-290 (propane), and R-441A have been approved for use in small appliances. All of these refrigerants are flammable and carry an A3 rating. Observe the following safety precautions when working with hydrocarbons:

▶ Never expose HC refrigerant cylinders to open flame or other high heat sources.

▶ Never do any cutting, brazing, or welding on units that contain HC refrigerants.

▶ Take care to prevent concentrations of any HC refrigerant above the lower flammability limit that would allow the refrigerant to ignite if exposed to an ignition source.

▶ Never use oxygen to purge or pressurize an HC system.

▶ HC refrigerants are exempt from venting regulations. If an HC refrigerant is being recovered, the recovery machine must be UL-listed for use with hydrocarbons and both the system and the recovery machine must be properly grounded.

REFRIGERANT CYLINDERS

Disposable cylinders Virgin refrigerants are usually packaged in disposable containers for use by air conditioning and refrigeration service personnel. Disposable cylinders are manufactured in sizes that include 20-lb, 30-lb, and 50-lb capacities. Disposable cylinders are meant for one-time use and may not be refilled or utilized for any other purpose. Any refrigerant remaining in a cylinder must be recovered to a level of 0 psig before disposal of the cylinder. After recovery, cylinders should be opened and rendered useless and the metal then should be recycled.

At the present time, refrigerant manufacturers and packagers voluntarily color-code cylinders. Colors are assigned per AHRI Guideline N, but note that color shades may vary somewhat

Refrigerant	Color	Refrigerant	Color	Refrigerant	Color
R-11	Orange	R-124	Deep green	R-407C	Medium brown
R-12	White	R-125	Medium brown	R-410A	Rose
R-13	Light blue	R-134a	Light blue	R-500	Yellow
R-22	Light green	R-401A	Pinkish red	R-502	Light purple
R-23	Light blue gray	R-401B	Yellow brown	R-503	Aqua
R-113	Dark purple	R-402A	Light brown	R-507	Teal
R-114	Dark blue	R-402B	Green brown	As of 2020:	
R-123	Light blue gray	R-404A	Orange	All	Light green gray

AHRI Guideline N: Refrigerant cylinder color codes

among manufacturers. Be aware, too, that a recent update to Guideline N calls for all refrigerant containers to have one uniform paint color—a light green gray—by 2020, with markings and labels used to identify the container's contents.

Regulations Disposable cylinders are manufactured to specifications established by the U.S. Department of Transportation (DOT), which has regulatory authority over all hazardous materials in commercial transportation. Disposable cylinders must adhere to Specification 39. These one-trip (non-reusable, non-refillable) cylinders, therefore, are often referred to as "DOT-39s" (see illustration next page).

Cylinder pressure Cylinders can become overpressurized for several reasons, primarily overheating. When temperatures rise, the compressed gas expands and can liquid-fill the cylinder. This is known as a *hydrostatic* condition. When a cylinder reaches a hydrostatic

GENERAL KNOWLEDGE

condition, the internal pressure rises very rapidly with even minor increases in temperature. If the safety relief device is unable to vent the increased pressure adequately, the cylinder could explode, causing property damage, personal injury, or even death. *Never tamper with a cylinder safety device or overfill a cylinder.*

A cylinder also can become overpressurized if it is connected to the discharge side of a refrigeration or air conditioning system. In such cases, the compressor can create pressures greater than the capacity of the safety relief device on the cylinder.

Typical DOT-39 disposable cylinder

Hazards of reuse

Disposable cylinders are manufactured from steel. Rust can eventually weaken the cylinder to the point at which the wall can no longer contain the compressed gas. Cylinders must be stored and transported in dry environments. Cylinders exhibiting extreme rust should be emptied of their contents and properly discarded.

Every refrigerant cylinder is silk-screened with product, safety, and warning information. This information, as well as information available in manufacturer's technical bulletins and the product's Safety Data Sheet (SDS), should be read carefully and followed.

Manufacturers of DOT-39 cylinders have switched to a one-way valve design, which allows the refrigerant to be removed, but prevents the cylinder from being refilled. A green valve handle identifies these newer cylinders (older cylinders had a black valve handle). Transportation of refilled DOT-39 cylinders is illegal and subject to a penalty of up to $25,000 in fines and five years of imprisonment.

Disposal All refrigerants should be properly recovered from empty disposable cylinders. The cylinder can be punctured with the valve open. Used cylinders can be recycled with your scrap metal dealer. Never leave used cylinders with residual product outdoors or at a job site. The internal pressure of a cylinder containing one ounce of liquid refrigerant is exactly the same as that of a full cylinder. An abandoned cylinder will eventually deteriorate—and potentially rupture if the cylinder wall weakens before the safety device activates.

Safety guidelines The following safety guidelines apply to *all* cylinders:

- *Never* drop a cylinder or hit it with a hammer or any other tool.

- *Never* apply live steam or direct flame to a cylinder.

- Do not lift a cylinder by its valve cover or valve. Never remove a valve from a cylinder or attempt to repair it.

- Do not tamper with the cylinder's safety device.

- *Never* refill disposable cylinders.

- Do not remove or attempt to alter any permanent cylinder markings (it is illegal to do so).

- Be careful not to dent, cut, scratch, or otherwise damage any cylinder or valve.

- Protect cylinders from moisture, salt, and corrosive chemicals or a corrosive atmosphere in any form.

- Always open valves slowly, and close after each use.

- Do not attempt to use a cylinder in a rusted or otherwise deteriorated condition. Contact appropriate personnel for disposal.

Disposable cylinders may be used for shipping virgin refrigerant only. They are never permitted for any further use.

OSHA (Occupational Safety and Health Administration) requires that compressed gas cylinders be used *only* by individuals who are trained in the proper handling and safe use of such cylinders.

Recovery cylinders

Recovery cylinders are reusable tanks that are built to a higher standard and constructed of a heavier material than disposable (DOT-39) cylinders. Recovery cylinders are identified as "refillable" and as such must meet all DOT standards for safety. Refrigerant recovery tanks can be identified by color—the body of the cylinder is painted gray, and the top is yellow. These tanks must be inspected and hydrostatically tested every five years to ensure that they can be used safely under pressure. The last test date (month and year) will be stamped on the top of the tank.

Typical recovery cylinder

Before a recovery tank is used, it should be inspected for damage, such as dents, rust, or corrosion. Always make sure that the tank is within the 5-year inspection period. The tank should be evacuated before use and should always be labeled to identify the refrigerant in the tank to prevent the mixing of different refrigerants. Cylinders should be secured during recovery and during transportation to prevent damage to the tank or release of the refrigerant.

Cylinder collar

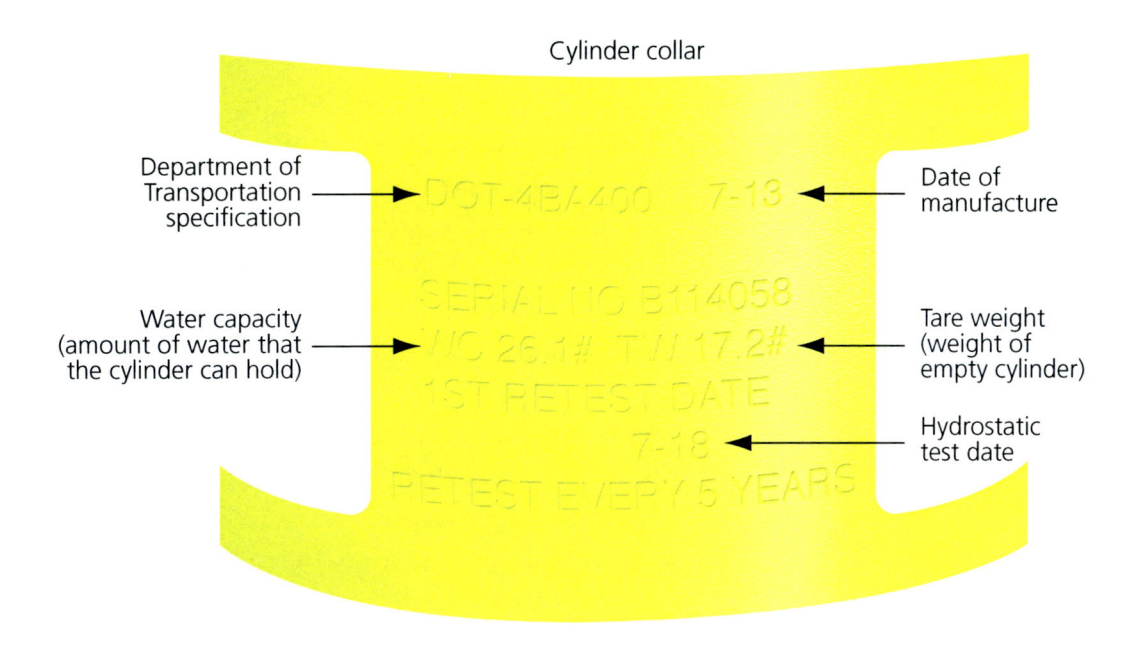

Department of Transportation specification → DOT-4BA400   7-13 ← Date of manufacture

SERIAL NO B114058
Water capacity (amount of water that the cylinder can hold) → WC 26.1# TW 17.2# ← Tare weight (weight of empty cylinder)
1ST RETEST DATE
7-18 ← Hydrostatic test date
RETEST EVERY 5 YEARS

Various information, including serial number and date of manufacture, is stamped on the top of the cylinder. Cylinder capacity is shown as "WC" (water capacity). The WC figure identifies the amount of water, by weight, that the cylinder will hold when full. This number will be very close to its capacity for refrigerant, but the density of water and of the refrigerant must be used for a full calculation. *A cylinder must never be filled beyond 80% of its capacity.* The extra space remaining in the cylinder allows for the expansion of the refrigerant if the temperature increases. Without the space reserved for expansion, a slight increase in temperature can cause a drastic increase in hydrostatic pressure within the tank, which in turn can cause the tank to rupture.

Various methods are used to ensure that tanks are not filled to more than the 80% capacity. A tank may be equipped with a float device that connects into the recovery machine to shut off the machine automatically at the 80% level. Some electronic scales have electronic shutoff devices that close the valve when the designated weight is reached. Most of the time, technicians use the gross weight of the cylinder to determine the fill level. By measuring the actual weight of the filled cylinder and subtracting the *tare weight*, which is the weight of the empty cylinder, you can determine how much refrigerant is in the tank. The tare weight will be listed on the top of the tank.

GENERAL KNOWLEDGE

Never mix one refrigerant with another type of refrigerant. Many common refrigerants form azeotropes with other refrigerants. These mixtures may be impossible to separate, and consequently must be destroyed rather than reclaimed.

Use personal protective equipment when filling and handling cylinders. This includes side-shield glasses, gloves, and safety shoes. Avoid skin contact with liquid refrigerant.

Be aware that inhaling high concentrations of any refrigerant vapor is harmful. It may cause heart irregularities, loss of consciousness, or death. Since vapor is heavier than air, avoid low areas without suitable ventilation. *Always exercise extreme caution when moving cylinders.*

Never apply a torch or open flame to a refrigerant cylinder. Doing so can result in permanent damage to the cylinder and an uncontrolled rise in tank pressure, which in turn can cause:

▶ the tank to explode, leading to serious injury and property damage

▶ the tank's relief valve to open, allowing the refrigerant to be vented to the atmosphere

▶ the refrigerant in the tank to decompose into toxic materials.

Do not fill a recovery cylinder that is out of date. The present date cannot be more than five years past the test date that you see stamped on the cylinder. The test date will look something like the example shown in the illustration on the next page. The designation in this example tells you that the cylinder was retested in October 2016 by retester number B732. If a cylinder is out of date—as the one in the example above would be after October 2021—it must not be filled. Promptly return it to the cylinder owner for retesting.

After filling, it is important to verify that all cylinder valves are closed properly. This prevents leaks during subsequent handling and shipment. If necessary, leak test the valves using soapy water.

Shipping procedures

The Department of Transportation (DOT) has jurisdiction over shipping. All cylinders used to transport refrigerants must meet DOT standards.

The EPA does not characterize used refrigerants as hazardous waste. Most states share this view and, as a result, require no special procedures for used refrigerant shipments. However, individual states can make regulations that are stricter than the federal rules. You should always check the local jurisdiction for special requirements, and be aware that the following general information is not to be considered complete for shipping used refrigerants that *are* classified as hazardous waste.

The reclaimer you select will be able to supply you with specific information on shipping your recovered refrigerant. Most will also supply the required labels and forms. All used refrigerant containers must be properly labeled. Cylinders and drums should be labeled *prior* to filling. Never fill a cylinder or drum that is not labeled for that material. The labels help prevent the accidental mixing of refrigerants, enable the service company to track quantities of each refrigerant for record-keeping purposes, and allow the reclaimer to identify the contents easily. Unlabeled containers in your truck could be dangerous and illegal. In the event of an accident, most emergency personnel are instructed to avoid unidentified containers or cylinders. They must wait for a hazardous materials response team to arrive and identify the contents of the containers. This can cause unnecessary delays.

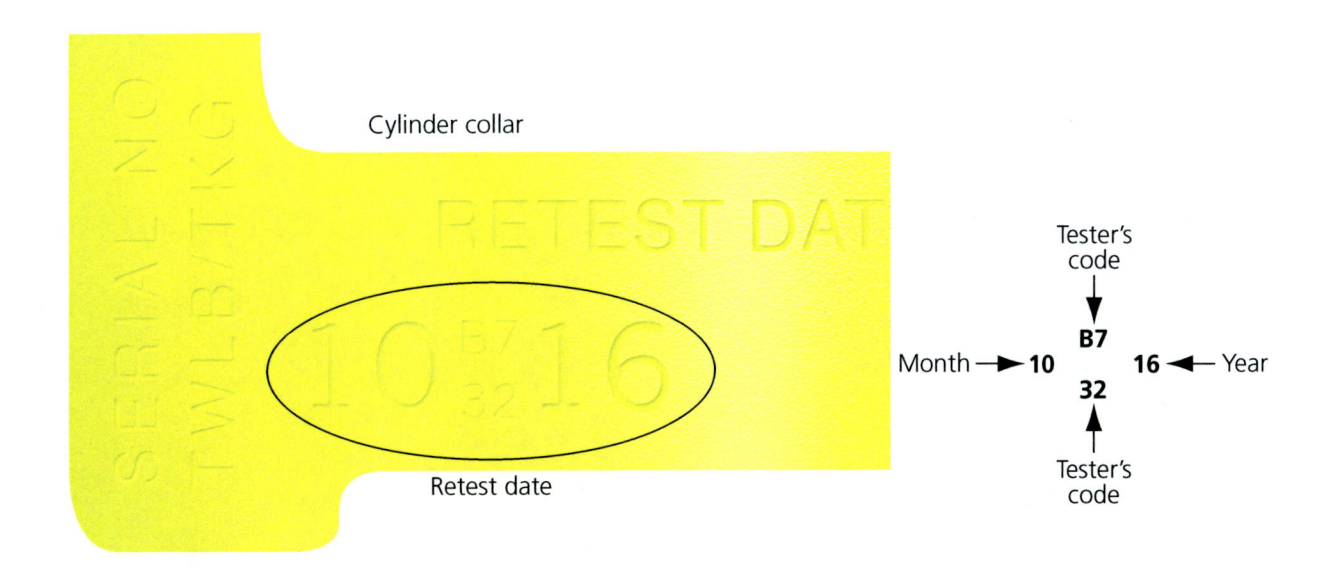

Cylinder collar

Retest date

Month → 10   Tester's code ↓ **B7**   **16** ← Year
              32 ↑ Tester's code

GENERAL KNOWLEDGE 53

The following is a summary of typical requirements and procedures: Apply the appropriate used refrigerant label to the shoulder of each cylinder. If the label on the cylinder is illegible, remove it completely and apply a new label. The CAS (Chemical Abstracts Service) number and UN/NA (United Nations/North American) identification number must always be shown. Next, install the gold hood cap over the cylinder valve. Complete a used refrigerant identification tag for each cylinder. Attach this tag to the gold hood cap with a plastic tie. Complete a green DOT classification tag for each cylinder. Attach the tag to the gold hood cap with a plastic tie. All cylinders are to be shipped in the upright position. Finally, complete the bill of lading. The following information generally is required:

- company name of carrier
- date
- company name and address of shipper
- signature of shipping company's representative
- shipping destination
- identity of refrigerant (R-134a, R-410A, etc.) and UN/NA number
- number of containers of each gas being shipped
- gross product weight, in pounds
- shipping information.

The illustration on the next page shows some examples of various labels and tags.

R-134a

CH$_2$FCF$_3$
1,1,1,2-tetrafluoroethane
CAS number 811-97-2
2.2, UN3159

NON-FLAMMABLE GAS 2

REFRIGERANT EVACUATION CERTIFICATION TAG

CONTAINS NO CFCs   ENVIRONMENTALLY SAFE
THIS UNIT COMPLIES WITH SECTION 608 OF THE CLEAN AIR ACT

Date of evacuation _____

Replacement refrigerant type _____

Replacement oil used _____

Unit evacuated by_____
          Certified technician

Servicing company_____

Address _____

Phone _____

Evacuated units owner _____

Address _____

_____

Phone _____

Date _____

Recovery Cylinder Identification

Company name _____
City/State _____
Customer/Contractor _____
Address _____
Phone _____

Cylinder contains   ☐ R-22   ☐ R-134a   ☐ R-410A   ☐ Other _____

Cylinder size   ☐ 30 lb   ☐ 40 lb   ☐ 50 lb   ☐ 125 lb

Pressure rating (psig)   ☐ 240/260   ☐ 300/350   ☐ 400

Cylinder Serial No. _____   Gross weight _____

Tare weight _____   Net weight _____

Attach to cylinder   # ___ of ___   Initials _____

Examples of typical labels and tags

GENERAL KNOWLEDGE

TYPE I

Small Appliances

THE TYPE I SECTION OF THIS STUDY GUIDE is designed to help technicians understand the information necessary for obtaining Type I certification. The Type I classification certifies technicians for refrigerant service of small appliances. The EPA restricts the sale of refrigerants to EPA-certified technicians. The EPA defines a small appliance as:

> *Any appliance that is fully manufactured, charged, and hermetically sealed in a factory with 5 lb or less of refrigerant, including, but not limited to, refrigerators and freezers (designed for home, commercial, or consumer use), medical or industrial research refrigeration equipment, room air conditioners (including window air conditioners, portable air conditioners, and packaged terminal air heat pumps), dehumidifiers, under-the-counter ice makers, vending machines, and drinking water coolers.*

It is recommended that this section be studied if you are attempting a Universal certification, or if you are taking or retaking the Type I exam. In addition to relevant material from the Core section, you should study the following information, which is unique to Type I.

DEFINITIONS

The EPA definition of a "small" appliance quoted on the previous page limits the type of equipment included in Type I certification. Central air conditioning systems, MVAC-like equipment, and commercial refrigeration equipment are *not* included in Type I, even though they may contain less than 5 lb of refrigerant. A few further definitions may be helpful at this point:

▶ **Appliance.** Any device that contains and uses a Class I (CFC) or Class II (HCFC) substance or substitute (e.g., HFC) as a refrigerant and which is used for household or commercial purposes, including any air conditioner, motor vehicle air conditioner, refrigerator, chiller, or freezer.

▶ **MVAC-like appliance.** Any mechanical vapor compression, open-drive compressor appliance with a full charge of 20 lb or less of refrigerant used to cool the driver's or passenger's compartment of an off-road motor vehicle. This includes, but is not limited to, the air conditioning equipment found in agricultural or construction vehicles. This definition is not intended to cover appliances using R-22.

▶ **Technician.** Any person who in the course of maintenance, service, or repair of an appliance could be reasonably expected to violate the integrity of the refrigerant circuit and therefore release refrigerants into the environment. "Technician" also means any person who disposes of an appliance that could be reasonably expected to violate the integrity of the refrigerant circuit and therefore release refrigerants from the appliance into the environment, except for persons who dispose only appliances that are small appliances, MVACs, and MVAC-like appliances. Activities reasonably expected to violate the integrity of the refrigerant circuit include, but are not limited to, attaching and detaching hoses and gauges to and from the appliance, adding or removing refrigerant, adding or removing components, and cutting the refrigerant line. Activities such as painting the appliance, rewiring an external electric circuit, replacing insulation on a length of pipe, or tightening nuts and bolts are not reasonably expected to violate the integrity of the refrigerant circuit. Activities conducted on appliances that have been properly evacuated pursuant to 82.156 are not reasonably expected to release refrigerants unless the activity includes adding refrigerant to the appliance. "Technicians" could include, but are not limited to, installers, contractor employees, in-house service personnel, and in some cases owners and/or operators of appliances.

▶ **Major repair, maintenance or service.** Any service involving the removal of any or all of the following components: compressor, condenser, evaporator, or auxiliary heat exchanger coil.

It is important to note the reference to the system being "hermetically sealed." Small appliance systems do not require service connections, but must have some type of service aperture. This usually takes the form of a straight piece of tubing (process tube), which can be used for connection with piercing access valves. Access valves must be checked for leaks after they have been installed and before the refrigerant has been recovered. These valves must be removed after repairs are completed and before recharging takes place, since they have a tendency to leak after a period of equipment operation. The illustration below shows a common line-piercing valve.

Small appliances have few leaks, since they are hermetically sealed at the factory. Nevertheless, appliances should be checked visually for leaks (look for any sign of oil) before you start the recovery process. Since these systems fall below the 50-lb threshold, there is no requirement that leaves be repaired—however, it is highly recommended. If the gauges read 0 psig (atmospheric pressure) when initially connected to the system, do not attempt to recover any refrigerant. Doing so will result only in pumping noncondensibles into the recovery vessel.

RECOVERY

Before beginning a refrigerant recovery procedure, *always* make sure to identify the refrigerant that is in the system and in the recovery tank. Mixtures of different types of refrigerants in one cylinder may cost extra to process or even be refused at the reclaim center. Some older refrigerators or freezers may contain non-fluorocarbon refrigerants, which must not be recovered with current recovery equipment. The same is true for many recreational vehicle appliances, both old and new.

New hydrocarbon (flammable) refrigerants such as R-600a, R-441A, and R-290 have been approved by the EPA for use in domestic refrigerators and other small appliances. (R-450A is a non-flammable refrigerant that also has been approved for domestic refrigerators.) Recovery machines should not be used for hydrocarbon refrigerants unless the recovery equipment is UL-certified for that purpose. Certain hydrocarbon refrigerants—specifically, R-600a, R-441A, R-290, and R-170—have been exempted by the EPA from the venting prohibition. Note that hydrocarbon refrigerants are *not* approved for retrofit into any system. Some other "natural" refrigerants, such as very high pressure R-744 (carbon dioxide), are also exempt from the venting prohibition.

Recovery of refrigerant from a small appliance may be carried out in either of two ways—with passive (system-dependent) recovery equipment, or with self-contained recovery equipment.

Passive (system-dependent) recovery equipment requires the assistance of components contained within the appliance to remove the refrigerant. The refrigerant must be recovered into a non-pressurized container. *Never* use a vacuum pump for any type of refrigerant recovery. A vacuum pump only pumps vapor at atmospheric pressure or lower.

Self-contained recovery equipment is equipment capable of removing the refrigerant from an appliance without the assistance of components contained within the appliance. Technicians who work only on small appliances are not required to have self-contained recovery units, since these systems contain less than 5 lb of refrigerant. However, self-contained recovery units will significantly speed up the recovery process.

Techniques

A recovery cylinder should be evacuated to 500 microns before initial use. Properly label the recovery cylinder with the type of refrigerant being reclaimed. *Never* mix different refrigerants in the same cylinder. You must allow a cylinder to reach a known (room) temperature before you can obtain an accurate pressure reading. A pressure above the known temperature-pressure relationship indicates that excessive air or other noncondensibles are present in the cylinder. The presence of noncondensibles also can cause excessive pressure to occur on the high side of the recovery machine during the recovery process. Refrigerant in a contaminated cylinder should be turned in for reclaim and must not be reused.

Remember: *Always* verify the type of refrigerant in the appliance. While the EPA recognizes many replacement refrigerants, it does not recognize any as "drop-ins".

Requirements

When recovering refrigerant with system-dependent equipment, you must be able to recover at least 80% of the charge if the compressor is not operating, or evacuate to a 4-in. vacuum. Recover the refrigerant from both the high and low sides of the system. This will ensure complete recovery and speed the process. It is more likely for refrigerant to become trapped in the compressor oil when passive recovery equipment is used. Consequently, extra steps should be taken to release the refrigerant. Warming the compressor oil and tapping the compressor with a rubber hammer will help release refrigerant from the oil. Energizing the defrost heaters on a frost-free refrigerator or freezer can decrease recovery time.

If the compressor is operating, at least 90% of the charge must be recovered, or a 4-in. vacuum must be reached. Run the compressor and recover the refrigerant from the high side.

Remember to check your recovery equipment, including the gauge manifold and hoses, for leaks on a regular basis.

A pungent odor or signs of contamination in the oil during the recovery or repair process may indicate a compressor burnout, which will require additional cleanup to flush out the contaminants. Nitrogen (an inert gas) should be used to purge air from the system before and during brazing. Nitrogen also should be used to pressurize the system for leak-testing. If leaks cannot be found with nitrogen alone, a trace amount of the system's refrigerant can be added to the nitrogen for leak detection. Nitrogen that has been introduced into the system may be vented to atmosphere.

The EPA allows the use of either passive or system-dependent recovery equipment on systems that contain less than 15 lb of refrigerant. Any system that contains more than 15 lb of refrigerant must use a self-contained recovery machine. New recovery equipment must meet the following EPA requirements:

▶ It must be tested by an EPA-approved third party.

▶ It must be equipped with low-loss fittings.

▶ If it is to be used with a flammable refrigerant, it must meet specific UL safety standards.

▶ Gauge hoses used with the recovery equipment also must have low-loss fittings, which may include self-sealing fittings or hand valves.

REFRIGERATION CYCLE

The diagram on page 29 in the Core section of this book illustrates a basic refrigeration cycle. Be aware that a small appliance as defined under Type I classification does not use a receiver or the type of suction accumulator shown. The normal high-side connection for a small appliance is a process tube at the outlet of the condenser. The normal low-side connection is a low-pressure process tube on the hermetic compressor, or the suction line close to the compressor.

SAFETY

When you are working with refrigerants, safety goggles or glasses and butyl-lined gloves are necessary attire. As noted, nitrogen is the recommended inert gas for leak-checking a system. A regulator must be used on the nitrogen cylinder to control the amount of pressure applied to the appliance.

Because refrigerants are heavier than air, a large leak or accidental release of refrigerant can displace the oxygen in the work area. The area should be evacuated immediately and ventilated with fresh air to remove the refrigerant. High temperatures, normally from an open flame, can cause the refrigerant to decompose, forming hydrofluoric and hydrochloric acids and phosgene gas. Before using cylinders that are equipped with Schrader valves, inspect any such valve for a damaged core. Make sure that a cap is installed whenever connections are not applied.

Never fill a recovery tank beyond 80% of its capacity. (This precaution allows for the expansion of the refrigerant as the temperature increases.) The tank can be weighed with a scale, or a float can be used inside the tank to prevent overfilling.

Charging cylinders with graduated markings normally are filled with liquid at the valve connection located at the lowest point (bottom) of the cylinder. The vapor released from the upper (top) valve connection must be recovered. The release of vapor to the atmosphere is prohibited.

HC refrigerants now being used in small appliances are flammable and require special handling. Technicians should acquire additional training related to HC refrigerants prior to working on these systems. Household refrigerators that use HC refrigerants will have safety markings in several locations:

- ▶ on or near the evaporator or exposed refrigerant tubing

- ▶ near the machine compartment

- ▶ on the exterior of the refrigerator.

TYPE II

High-Pressure Systems

THE TYPE II SECTION OF THIS STUDY GUIDE is designed to help technicians understand the information necessary for obtaining Type II certification. The Type II classification certifies technicians for refrigerant service of high-pressure and very high-pressure appliances. The EPA defines a high-pressure appliance as:

> *Any appliance that uses a refrigerant with a liquid-phase saturation pressure between 170 psia and 355 psia at 104°F. Examples include but are not limited to appliances using R-22, R-407C, R-410A, and R-502.*

The EPA defines a very high-pressure appliance as:

> *Any appliance that uses a refrigerant with a critical temperature below 104°F, or with a liquid-phase saturation pressure above 355 psia at 104°F. Examples include but are not limited to appliances using R-13, R-23, R-503, R-508A, and R-508B.*

It is recommended that this section be studied if you are attempting a Universal certification, or if you are taking or retaking the Type II exam. In addition to relevant material from the Core section, you should study the following information, which is unique to Type II.

EQUIPMENT CATEGORIES

Comfort cooling is defined as air conditioning appliances used to provide cooling in order to control heat and/or humidity in facilities including, but not limited to, office buildings and commercial buildings. Comfort cooling appliances include building chillers and self-contained rooftop units. They may be used for the comfort of occupants or for climate control to protect equipment within a facility, including but not limited to computer rooms.

Commercial cooling is defined as refrigeration appliances used in the retail food and cold storage warehouse sectors. Retail food includes the refrigeration equipment found in supermarkets, convenience stores, restaurants, and other food service establishments. Cold storage includes the refrigeration equipment used to store meat, produce, dairy products, and other perishable goods.

Industrial process refrigeration is defined as complex customized appliances that are directly linked to the processes used in, for example, the chemical, pharmaceutical, petrochemical, and manufacturing industries. This sector also includes industrial ice machines, ice rinks, and appliances used directly in the generation of electricity.

For cases in which one appliance is used for both industrial process refrigeration and other applications, the appliance will be considered industrial process refrigeration equipment if 50% or more of its operating capacity is used for industrial process refrigeration.

LEAK DETECTION

All high-pressure or very high-pressure appliances should be visually inspected for signs of oil when a leak is suspected. (Oil travels through the system with the refrigerant, and will leave traces wherever a large enough leak is present). The Core section of this book describes the various methods of leak detection (soap bubbles, electronic, ultrasonic, and dye) that have been approved by the EPA.

Open compressors used in the HVACR industry have an inherent tendency to leak at the shaft seal if the system has not been run for a long period of time. Excessive superheat on the suction side of the system is an indication of a leak. After installing a new built-up system or making repairs to an existing system, first pressurize the system with an inert gas (such as nitrogen) and test it for leaks. An ultrasonic leak detector can be used along with soap bubbles to pinpoint the exact location of any leaks. When the use of an inert gas is not sufficient for leak testing, a small amount of the system's design refrigerant may be added to the appliance as a trace gas.

Repair requirements

The EPA requires all industrial process systems containing more than 50 lb of refrigerant to be repaired if the leak rate exceeds 30% (effective 2019) of the total charge per year. All commercial refrigeration systems containing more than 50 lb of refrigerant must be repaired if the leak rate exceeds 20% (effective 2019) of the total charge per year. All comfort cooling systems containing more than 50 lb of refrigerant must be repaired if the leak rate exceeds 10% (effective 2019) of the total charge per year. Leaks exceeding allowable rates, with few exceptions, must be repaired within 30 days unless the machine is retired or mothballed. The 30-day period can be extended if government regulations make repairs impossible, if the area is subject to radiological contamination, or if the parts needed to make the repair are not available. Leak rates need to be calculated any time refrigerant is added, even when a repair has not been made. The equipment nameplate or manufacturer's specifications should be referenced to determine the full system charge.

If a leak in a system that contains 50 lb or more of refrigerant exceeds 125% of the total charge in a one-year period of time, a report must be submitted to the EPA describing efforts to identify leaks and make repairs to the system. If the leaking equipment cannot be repaired, the owner must develop a plan to retrofit or replace the equipment within one year. The one-year period can be extended to 18 months if the replacement uses a refrigerant that is exempt from venting, such as CO_2.

To "mothball" a machine means that the machine must be shut down and the refrigerant removed or isolated from the leak area.

The pressure in the machine must be brought down to 0 psig. This will extend the repair deadline but the machine cannot be put back on line until repairs are made.

VERIFICATION TESTING

After repairs are made, *verification testing* must be done to ensure that the leak rate has been brought below the threshold. All leak inspections must be performed by certified technicians. The initial verification test must be done before refrigerant is returned to the machine. Follow-up tests must be performed after the machine has been put back in service and at normal running conditions, but within 10 days. Additional repairs and testing may be conducted as needed within the 30-day repair window. Additional leak inspections must be made annually until the leak rate is below the threshold. In the case of industrial process refrigeration equipment containing more than 500 lb of refrigerant, the test must be done every three months. The owner is responsible for maintaining records of all leak inspections, leak repairs, and verification tests for a minimum of three years.

RECOVERY

Techniques

It is important for maintenance to be performed periodically on recovery machines. Oil and filters should be changed at properly scheduled intervals. Most small recovery units have air-cooled condensers that should be clean at all times. Larger recovery machines may have water-cooled condensers. The water supply for these condensers must be obtained from a local municipal source, not from the equipment. Any refrigerant left in the machine from the last recovery job must be recovered before connecting the machine to another appliance, and the filters also should be changed. The empty refillable cylinder must be evacuated with a vacuum pump prior to the recovery process.

The fastest method of recovery is to remove as much refrigerant as possible in the liquid phase. It is possible that some oil, moisture, and acids will be removed along with the liquid refrigerant. Inspect the system first in order to locate the proper place for the removal of liquid refrigerant. The liquid

Remove access valve cores for unrestricted flow

APPION INC.

line is generally the proper connection point. However, if the condenser is located below the evaporator or receiver, the connection should be at the condenser outlet. If the condenser is above the evaporator, recovery should begin from the liquid line entering the evaporator. Keep restrictions to a minimum by using hoses with the shortest length and largest diameter possible. Removing cores from Schrader valves also will help speed the recovery process. The illustration above shows a valve core removal tool.

The vapor remaining in the appliance must be recovered after the liquid refrigerant has been removed. Vapor recovery minimizes oil loss. Recovery time can be reduced by packing the recovery cylinder in ice or warming parts of the refrigeration system. Recovery equipment that uses a hermetic compressor as the pump may shut down before completing the process. This is due to the fact that some hermetic compressors on recovery machines are cooled by refrigerant flowing across the motor, and may overheat when pulling a deep vacuum because of a lack of refrigerant flow. Superheat in the vapor may prevent the vapor from cooling the motor. If you consistently work on larger equipment, a recovery machine that uses an oil-less compressor may be a wise investment.

When you make a major repair—described by the EPA as the replacement of a compressor, condenser, evaporator, or auxiliary heat exchanger—refrigerant recovery is required. When the system requires service and is equipped with a receiver, the refrigerant can be pumped into the receiver and isolated there during service. In other cases, the component that needs to be replaced (such as a compressor) can be isolated and only the section of the system to be opened will need to be recovered.

When recovering refrigerant, either from the entire system or from an isolated portion, be sure to follow the instructions of the recovery equipment manufacturer. Make sure that all hoses are connected properly and that all valves are in the proper position. In addition, check oil levels and filters on the machine as appropriate. After the system has been pulled down to the correct level, turn off the machine and allow the system to stand for a few minutes. A rise in pressure may indicate that there is still refrigerant in the system and the recovery process needs to continue. If there is no rise in pressure, the system is ready for repairs. If the system has significant leaks, it may be impossible to reach the required recovery level—in that case, the system should be recovered to 0 psig. The recovered refrigerant may be returned to the unit after repairs are made.

Requirements The EPA allows the use of passive (or "system-dependent") recovery equipment on systems containing less than 15 lb of refrigerant. Any system containing more than 15 lb must use a self-contained recovery machine. New recovery equipment must meet the following EPA requirements:

▶ It must be tested by an EPA-approved third party.

▶ It must be equipped with low-loss fittings.

▶ If it is to be used with flammable refrigerant, it must meet specific UL safety standards.

▶ Gauge hoses used with the recovery equipment also must have low-loss fittings, which can include self-sealing fittings or hand valves.

EPA regulations governing recovery equipment and vacuum standards are summarized in Table 1. It is imperative that service technicians who perform recovery procedures adhere to these regulations. Look back at page 21. As you can see, Table 1 shows acceptable vacuum levels according to the type of refrigerant and the amount of refrigerant in a system. (Leak regulations change at the 50-lb charge level and vacuum regulations change at the 200-lb charge level.) The date of manufacture of the recovery equipment determines the vacuum level that it must be capable of achieving.

Technicians are required to maintain records of disposed appliances containing 5 to 50 lb of refrigerant for a minimum of three years. The records must include the following: the company name, the location of the appliance, the date of recovery, the type of refrigerant recovered, the total quantity of refrigerant recovered in each calendar month, the quantity of refrigerant (by type) transferred for reclamation and/or destruction, the person to whom it was transferred, and the date of transfer.

REFRIGERATION CYCLE

The diagram on page 29 in the Core section of this book shows the major components of a high-pressure appliance (compressor, condenser, metering device, evaporator), plus a receiver and an accumulator. The location and function of each component are considered required knowledge for a HVACR service technician. The receiver is located in the high side of the system, after the condenser, when the metering device is a thermostatic expansion valve. A receiver is not used when the metering device is a capillary tube or fixed orifice. The refrigerant leaving the receiver is high-pressure liquid. A sight glass often is added to the liquid line to see if flashing is occurring, and many systems include a moisture indicator as well to help identify moisture issues in the refrigerant. The accumulator is located after the evaporator in the low side to collect any liquid refrigerant that may leave the evaporator, thus protecting the compressor.

A heater located in the crankcase of the compressor is designed to reduce the amount of refrigerant in the lubricating oil. An excessive amount of refrigerant in the oil can cause oil foaming in the crankcase and a loss of lubrication to the compressor parts. Many of the service valves installed on these appliances are back-seated valves. ("Back-seating" the valve closes off the gauge port, while "front-seating" closes the port to the compressor. The technician must be able to identify the direction of flow when the service valve stem is in a particular position.

Any time a system has been opened for repair, the filter-drier should be replaced and a deep vacuum must be pulled on the system. Filter-driers can remove moisture, solids, and acids from the running system. If the repairs are related to a compressor burnout, an oil sample should be taken to check for acid in the system. This will help determine necessary cleanup requirements.

Using a vacuum pump is the preferred way to remove moisture and noncondensibles from an appliance after repairs. The vacuum pump should be capable of pulling a vacuum of at least 500 microns. Noncondensibles left in the system will cause an increase in the high-side pressure and reduce system efficiency. It is possible that too large a vacuum pump may be used on an appliance. If this happens, the vacuum may reach the point at which water will freeze in the appliance before it can be removed. This will greatly increase the time needed to reach the desired vacuum. Nitrogen can be introduced during the vacuum to raise the pressure slightly and help reduce the possibility of freezing. Never start a hermetic compressor while it is under a deep vacuum—doing so can short out the motor windings and damage the compressor. The compressor also may be damaged if it is started with the discharge service valve closed.

Before recharging a system, check the equipment nameplate to verify the proper refrigerant and the proper charge. Be especially careful when you recharge systems that contain water-cooled condensers or chiller-type evaporators. After vapor has been added to increase the pressure of a given refrigerant above 32°F (36°F generally is recommended), the system can be charged with liquid through the liquid-line service valve. It is important to keep the circulating pumps of the water circuit running during the charging operation.

SAFETY

You should follow general safety practices, as covered in the Core section of this book, when performing service on any appliance. But be aware that many of the systems covered by

Type II are very large, and have different safety demands than small appliances do. The reciprocating compressors used on larger equipment may have service valves on both the suction and the discharge sides. The discharge-side service valve should never be front-seated while the compressor is in operation. The receiver of a Type II system must have a pressure relief device on it. These relief devices should never be connected in series. If greater capacity is needed, they may be connected in parallel. Sight glasses and viewing glasses may become covered with ice. An alcohol spray should be used to remove this ice (not a screwdriver!). *Remember: Think safety!*

Dry nitrogen frequently is used for breaking a vacuum in a system, for leak testing, and as an inert gas to prevent oxidation during brazing. Be mindful that the pressure in a nitrogen tank can do severe damage to a refrigeration system. Never use a nitrogen tank without a pressure regulator, and never pressurize a system beyond its low-side test pressure.

Systems in the Type II category with a charge of more than 50 lb are subject to ASHRAE Standard 15-2013. This standard requires a refrigerant-specific sensor (for all refrigerants) in the mechanical room to detect leaks, and also to initiate an alarm and start the ventilation system if the refrigerant level in the room exceeds the TLV-TWA for the given refrigerant. Refrigerant detectors are not required for ammonia (R-717) systems, which require continuous ventilation systems.

TYPE III

Low-Pressure Systems

THE TYPE III SECTION OF THIS STUDY GUIDE is designed to help technicians understand the information necessary for obtaining Type III certification. The Type III classification certifies technicians for refrigerant service of low-pressure appliances (centrifugal chillers). The EPA defines a low-pressure appliance as:

> *Any appliance that uses a refrigerant with a liquid-phase saturation pressure below 45 psia at 104°F. Examples include but are not limited to appliances using R-11, R-123, R-113, and R-245fa.*

It is recommended that this section be studied if you are attempting a Universal certification, or you are taking or retaking the Type III exam. But in addition to relevant material from the Core section, you should study the following information, which is unique to Type III.

LEAK DETECTION

Leak testing low-pressure systems involves considerations that are not present in equipment designed to operate at higher pressures. The EPA requires all industrial process systems containing more than 50 lb of refrigerant to be repaired if the leak rate exceeds 30% (effective 2019) of the total charge per year. All commercial refrigeration systems containing more than 50 lb of refrigerant must be repaired if the leak rate exceeds 20% (effective 2019) of the total charge per year. All comfort cooling systems containing more than 50 lb of refrigerant must be repaired if the leak rate exceeds 10% (effective 2019) of the total charge per year.

Note that if a machine is used for both comfort cooling and an industrial process application, the machine will be classified with the application that uses the greatest percentage of the load. For example, a machine that uses 30% of its capacity for comfort cooling and 70% of its capacity for the process application will be classified as belonging to the "industrial process refrigeration" category for the purpose of tracking trigger leak rates.

Leaks exceeding allowable rates, with few exceptions, must be repaired within 30 days unless the machine is retired or mothballed. The 30 days can be extended if government regulations make repairs impossible, if the area is subject to radiological contamination, or if the parts needed to make the repair are not available. Leak rates need to be calculated any time refrigerant is added, even when a repair has not been made. The equipment nameplate or manufacturer's specification should be referenced to determine the full system charge. If the leaking equipment cannot be repaired, the owner must develop a plan to retrofit or replace the equipment within one year. The one-year period can be extended to 18 months if the replacement uses a refrigerant that is exempt from venting, such as CO_2.

To "mothball" means that the machine must be shut down and the refrigerant removed or isolated from the leak area. The pressure in the machine must be brought down to 0 psig. This will extend the repair deadline but the machine cannot be put back on line until repairs are made.

ASHRAE Guideline 3 states that a system should be checked for leaks if, during a standing vacuum test beginning at 1 mm Hg (1,000 microns), the pressure rises to a level above 2.5 mm Hg (2,500 microns).

Low-pressure systems can be checked for leaks by adding nitrogen and preforming a standing pressure test. When using nitrogen in a low-pressure system, never exceed 10 psig. Low-pressure systems are protected against overpressure by a rupture disk at the evaporator. The rupture disk is designed to relieve pressure at 15 psig. Never raise the pressure beyond 10 psig, or the rupture disk could fail.

The best method of detecting leaks in a low-pressure machine is to raise the pressure in the system using the refrigerant already in the machine. Circulating warm water through the machine will warm the refrigerant and raise the pressure. Heat blanket systems (PREVAC) that serve the purpose are also available. Care must be taken to ensure that the pressure does not exceed 10 psig.

Purge units are necessary on low-pressure systems because the low side operates below atmospheric pressure and can draw in air (a noncondensible), mostly at gaskets and fittings. Leaks in the system admit more air, causing excessive operation of the purge system—which is often the first indication of leaks in the low side of the system. When the purge operates, a small amount of refrigerant is also discharged. To reduce this loss, the chiller should be leak tested and repaired as necessary. Excessive moisture collection in the purge unit can indicate a leak in the condenser or chiller barrel tubes.

The shell-and-tube evaporator (the "cooler") of a water chiller is where cooling takes place. Heat is absorbed by refrigerant in the shell, chilling the water flowing through the tubes. The tubes are secured into a tube sheet at each end. Water is supplied to the tubes, and collected from them, via cavities formed between the tube sheets and outside header caps. These cavities are called "water boxes." When the chiller is operating, any leak in the water tubes will cause water to leak from the tube into the shell. However, if the water flow is valved off and the water is drained, refrigerant in the shell will pass through the leak into the tubes, and will collect in the water boxes. Refrigerant then can be detected by inserting a leak detector probe through the drain valve in either of the water boxes.

Tubes in a low-pressure system may be checked for leaks using a hydrostatic tube test. This test involves blanking off the water side to isolate the machine from the rest of the system, filling the machine with water, and using a hand pump to raise the pressure in the machine. After allowing the machine to sit for a period of time, check the pressure in the machine. A drop in pressure indicates a leak in the tubes. If there is an indication of leaks, water should be drained prior to recovering refrigerant so that moisture is not pulled into the machine.

Open-drive compressors are less likely to be encountered today than they once were, but be aware that the shaft seals on open-drive compressors have the potential to be a significant source of leaks. If open-drive compressors are used, they should be checked regularly for leaks, and the seals will need to be changed periodically.

VERIFICATION TESTING

After repairs are made, *verification testing* must be done to ensure that the leak rate has been brought below the threshold. All leak inspections must be performed by certified technicians. The initial verification test must be done before refrigerant is returned to the machine. Follow-up tests must be performed after the machine has been put back in service and at normal running conditions, but within 10 days. Additional repairs and testing may be conducted as needed within the 30-day repair window. Additional leak inspections must be made annually until the leak rate is below the threshold. The owner is responsible for maintaining records of all leak inspections, leak repairs, and verification tests for a minimum of three years.

RECOVERY

Techniques Refrigerant must be recovered from the appliance any time the system has been opened for repairs. Major repairs include the replacement of evaporators, condensers, compressors, or heat exchangers. Some smaller repairs can be made by isolating refrigerant in parts of the machine that are not affected by the repair.

Oil samples often are taken at this time. If there has been a compressor burnout, the oil quality should be tested for acidity. Oil samples often are tested by the equipment manufacturer for the presence of different metals that can indicate internal wear on various parts of the machine.

Refrigerant is usually recovered from low-pressure chillers using a "push-pull" method that removes the liquid before recovering the vapor. The refrigerant should be removed from the appliance until a 25-mm vacuum has been achieved. The low level is needed because of the high boiling points of low-pressure refrigerants. After the required recovery level has been reached, the equipment should be shut off and allowed to stand for a few minutes to ensure that the pressure does not rise. The 25-mm recovery level also must be met before disposing of an appliance.

The high-pressure cut-out on a recovery unit must be set at 10 psig when you are removing refrigerant from a low-pressure

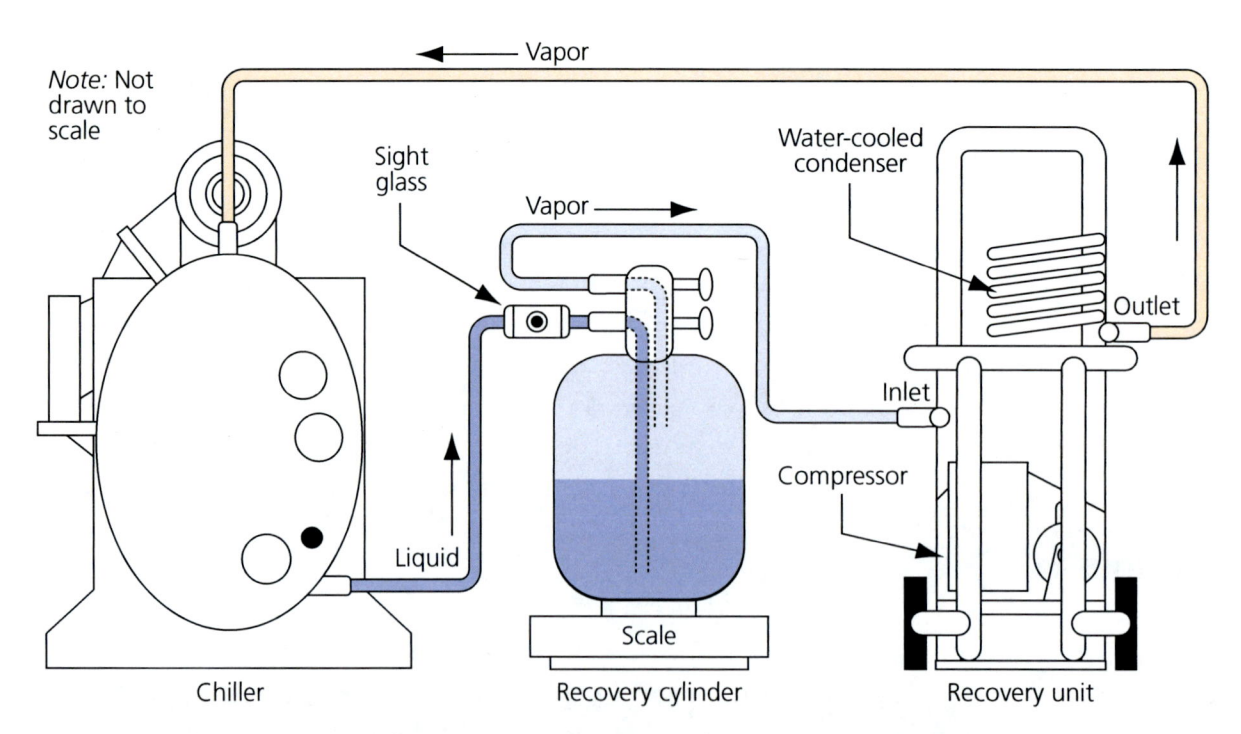

Liquid recovery from low-pressure system (type of recovery container may vary)

chiller (the low-pressure recovery vessel rupture disk relieves at 15 psig).

Recover liquid refrigerant first, then vapor. Removing the vapor after liquid recovery has been performed is important: a 350-ton R-11 chiller at 0 psig could still contain 100 lb of refrigerant in vapor form, even after the liquid refrigerant has been removed.

Heat can be used as a tool in recovering or recharging refrigerant in a low-pressure system. Oil will contain less refrigerant at higher temperatures (130 to 140°F suggested). If the oil is being removed from the machine, it too should be done at the higher temperature to drive out refrigerant before removal. When recovering refrigerant from chillers, remember to maintain water circulation to prevent freezing. In the case of a water-cooled recovery unit, this means that when vapor is being removed, the recovery unit's condenser water (usually from the municipal water supply) and the condenser and chilled water system pumps *all* should be on to prevent the water from freezing while the recovery pump is running.

The municipal water supply typically is used to cool the condenser on larger recovery machines due to its ability to absorb large amounts of heat and speed the recovery process. Increasing the temperature of the mechanical room where the chiller is located will raise the pressure in the machine to help speed the recovery process. Warming the chiller with warm water or cooling the recovery tanks also can speed up the recovery process.

Requirements EPA regulations include very specific requirements regarding the recovery of refrigerant from low-pressure systems. After the refrigerant removal procedure has been completed and the required recovery vacuum has been reached, some refrigerant could still exist in the system or in the oil. Wait at least a few minutes and check the system pressure for any rise, which could indicate that further recovery is necessary to attain the required evacuation level.

Systems do not need to be evacuated all the way to the required level if either of the following conditions applies:

▶ The service procedure does not qualify as "major" (see definition on page 60).

▶ Because of leaks, evacuation to the required level cannot be done or would contaminate the refrigerant being recovered.

In the first case—that of a non-"major" repair—the low-pressure system must be pressurized to 0 psig using a method such as controlled hot water, *not* a method that would require subsequent purging, such as adding nitrogen.

New recovery and recycling equipment must be labeled as certified to meet EPA requirements. These machines must be equipped with low-loss fittings and be capable of reaching the required 25-mm recovery level.

While low-pressure machines typically hold more than 50 lb of refrigerant, the technician must be aware of some newer rules relating to systems that have a charge between 5 and 50 lb of refrigerant. Disposal of appliances in this range now require the technician to maintain records of the disposal for a minimum of three years. The records must include:

▶ the company name

▶ the location of the appliance

▶ the date of recovery

▶ the type and amount of refrigerant recovered

▶ the quantity of refrigerant transferred for reclaim or disposal

▶ where and to whom it was transferred

▶ the date of the transfer.

RECHARGING TECHNIQUES

Prior to recharging, the system should be pulled into a deep vacuum of 500 microns. This level of vacuum ensures that all moisture has been removed and that the system is tight and free from leaks. If the refrigerant side contains significant amounts of moisture, nitrogen can be added to raise the pressure and help prevent the moisture from freezing. After the proper level of evacuation is met, the system should be allowed to sit idle for several minutes to check for a rise in pressure. A rise in pressure may indicate the presence of moisture or a leak.

This type of machine typically runs with a flooded evaporator, so refrigerant is added in the liquid state through the evaporator charging valve located near the bottom of the machine. Since large low-pressure systems are designed to chill water, charging methods must take the presence of water into consideration. Introducing liquid into a deep vacuum can cause the refrigerant to boil, and may lower temperatures enough to freeze water in the tubes. After service or repair of a low-pressure system, therefore, always charge in the *vapor* phase until the refrigerant saturation temperature increases to a point above 32°F. After that point, you may begin charging liquid refrigerant. A temperature-pressure chart should be used to determine the pressure for the refrigerant being charged (see the T-P charts on pages 86–87).

The recovery vessel being used to charge the vapor can be warmed with a heat blanket to increase the flow into the repaired system. The lowest access point on a low-pressure system is the evaporator charging valve.

REFRIGERATION CYCLE

A low-pressure system operates at a pressure below atmospheric, which means that air can be drawn into the machine through any leaks in the low side of the system. A purge unit therefore is required to remove noncondensibles from the system. The purge unit draws (takes its suction) from the top of the condenser, where noncondensibles get trapped. The purge unit condenses the refrigerant and returns it to the evaporator while venting the noncondensibles out of the machine. Newer high-efficiency purge units are equipped with their own small refrigeration units to lower the temperature further and condense more refrigerant, thus reducing the amount of refrigerant discharged along with the noncondensibles.

When a low-pressure system is idle for a long period of time, the system pressure should be maintained at a level slightly higher than atmospheric. This practice prevents unwanted air from entering the system through any leaks that may be present. The presence of air in an operating system normally is indicated by a higher-than-normal head pressure. If you use a vacuum pump that is too large, the pressure may drop so rapidly that water trapped in the system will freeze. If a smaller vacuum pump is not available, you may be able to use nitrogen with a regulator to increase the pressure enough to control this condition.

RETROFITS

Since CFCs have been eliminated and R-123 also is scheduled to be phased out (it is banned for use in new equipment as of 2020, and its production will stop in 2030), new alternative refrigerants are being considered. R-1233zd is one of the alternatives for R-123 that has SNAP approval. R-1233zd is non-flammable, has an A1 safety rating, and is suitable for use in large chillers. R-1233zd is also an HFO product with a low GWP (global warming potential) value. Other refrigerants also are being looked at for these applications.

SAFETY

Since low-pressure refrigerants remain in liquid form at atmospheric pressure and relatively high temperatures, specific safety precautions must be observed. *Never* attempt to siphon refrigerant by mouth, and avoid spilling it on exposed skin. Observe all requirements for safe handling, including the use of non-permeable gloves and eye protection (glasses or goggles) when working with refrigerants.

Precautions for the safety of the system also must be observed. Never install pressure relief valves in series. If ice forms on the outside of the system sight glass(es), remove it with an alcohol spray. Do *not* scrape or chip ice away with any tool. The rupture disk in the evaporator is set to open at 15 psig. The discharge of this disk should be piped to the outdoors, not to anywhere inside the building.

The typical chiller in the Type III category will have a refrigerant charge that well exceeds the 50-lb threshold, which means that the mechanical room will need to meet ASHRAE Standard 15-2013. This standard requires a refrigerant-specific sensor (for all refrigerants) in the mechanical room to detect leaks, and also to initiate an alarm and start the ventilation system if the refrigerant level in the room exceeds the TLV-TWA for the given refrigerant.

	Low-pressure refrigerants					Medium-pressure refrigerants		
Temp (°F)	CFC R-11	CFC R-113	CFC R-115	HCFC R-123	HFC R-245fa	HFO R-1233zd	CFC R-12	HCFC R-124	HFC R-134a
−50	* 28.8			* 29.2	* 14.1		* 15.4		* 18.6
−40	* 28.3		*1.2	* 28.8	* 13.9	* 28.3	* 11.0	* 22.1	* 14.7
−35	* 28.0		1.3	* 28.6	* 13.7	* 28.0	* 8.4	* 20.9	* 12.3
−30	* 27.7	* 29.3	3.4	* 28.3	* 13.5	* 27.6	* 5.5	* 19.4	* 9.7
−25	* 27.4	* 29.2	5.6	* 28.1	* 13.2	* 27.2	* 2.3	* 17.9	* 6.8
−20	* 26.9	* 29.1	8.1	* 27.7	* 13.0	* 26.7	0.6	* 16.0	* 3.6
−15	* 26.5	* 28.9	10.8	* 27.3	* 12.7	* 26.1	2.5	* 14.0	0.0
−10	* 25.9	* 28.7	13.7	* 26.9	* 12.2	* 25.5	4.5	* 11.8	2.0
−5	* 25.3	* 28.5	16.9	* 26.4	* 11.9	* 24.7	6.7	* 9.3	4.1
0	* 24.6	* 28.2	20.3	* 25.8	* 11.4	* 23.9	9.2	* 6.6	6.5
5	* 23.9	* 27.9	24.1	* 25.2	* 11.0	* 23.0	11.8	* 3.6	9.1
10	* 23.0	* 27.6	28.1	* 24.5	* 10.4	* 22.0	14.7	* 0.3	12.0
15	* 22.1	* 27.2	32.4	* 23.7	* 9.5	* 20.8	17.7	1.6	15.1
20	* 21.0	* 26.8	37.0	* 22.8	* 9.1	* 19.5	21.1	3.6	18.4
25	* 19.8	* 26.3	42.0	* 21.8	* 8.0	* 18.1	24.6	5.7	22.1
30	* 18.5	* 25.8	47.4	* 20.7	* 7.5	* 16.5	28.5	8.0	26.1
35	* 17.1	* 25.2	53.1	* 19.5	* 6.8	* 14.7	32.6	10.5	30.4
40	* 15.5	* 24.5	59.1	* 18.1	* 5.6	* 12.8	37.0	13.2	35.0
45	* 13.8	* 23.8	65.6	* 16.6	* 4.2	* 10.7	41.7	16.1	40.0
50	* 12.0	* 22.9	72.5	* 15.0	* 2.8	* 8.3	46.7	19.3	45.4
55	* 9.9	* 22.2	79.8	* 13.1	* 1.8	* 5.8	52.1	22.7	51.2
60	* 7.7	* 21.0	87.6	* 11.2	0.0	* 3.0	57.8	26.3	57.4
65	* 5.3	* 19.9	95.8	* 9.0	1.9	0.0	63.8	30.2	64.0
70	* 2.7	* 18.7	104.5	* 6.6	3.5	1.6	70.2	34.4	71.1
75	0.1	* 17.3	113.8	* 4.1	5.9	3.4	77.0	38.9	78.6
80	1.6	* 15.9	123.5	* 1.3	7.9	5.3	84.2	43.7	86.7
85	3.2	* 14.3	133.8	0.9	10.2	7.3	91.7	48.8	95.2
90	4.9	* 12.5	144.6	2.5	12.8	9.5	99.7	54.3	104.3
95	6.8	* 10.6	156.0	4.2	15.8	11.9	108.2	60.1	113.9
100	8.8	* 8.6	168.0	6.1	19.0	14.4	117.0	66.2	124.1
105	10.9	* 6.4	180.7	8.1	23.0	17.1	126.4	72.7	134.9
110	13.2	* 4.0	193.9	10.2	26.0	20.0	136.2	79.6	146.3
115	15.7	* 1.4	207.9	12.6	30.0	23.1	146.5	86.9	158.4
120	18.3	0.7	222.5	15.0	33.0	26.5	157.3	94.6	171.1
125	21.1	2.2	237.9	17.7	36.0	30.0	168.6	103.0	184.5
130	24.0	3.7	254.0	20.5	41.0	33.8	180.5	111.0	198.7
135	27.1	5.4	270.9	23.5	46.0	37.8	192.9	120.0	213.5
140	30.5	7.2	288.5	26.7	52.0	42.0	205.9	130.0	229.2
145	34.0	9.2	307.6	30.2	57.0	46.5	219.5	140.0	245.6
150	37.7	11.2	327.3	33.8	61.0	51.3	233.7	150.0	262.8

Pressures are shown as psig, except (*) indicates inches of mercury vacuum.

Temperature-pressure chart

Note: For R-404A, R-407A, and R-407C, use dew point values (temperatures 50°F and below) to determine superheat. Use bubble point values (temperatures above 50°F, with yellow background) to determine subcooling.

Temp (°F)	Medium-pressure refrigerants			High-pressure refrigerants					
	CFC R-500	HFO R-1234yf	HFO R-1234ze	HCFC R-22	HFC R-404A	HFC R-407A	HFC R-407C	HFC R-410A	CFC R-502
−50	* 12.8	* 15.6	* 21.9	* 6.1				5.0	* 0.2
−40	* 7.6	* 11.5	* 19.1	0.6	4.3	* 1.0	* 4.6	10.8	4.1
−35	* 4.6	* 8.9	* 17.4	2.6	6.8	1.0	* 0.9	14.0	6.5
−30	* 1.2	* 6.0	* 15.4	4.9	9.6	3.3	1.6	17.8	9.2
−25	1.2	* 2.8	* 13.3	7.5	12.7	5.8	3.9	21.9	12.1
−20	3.2	0.4	* 10.9	10.2	16.0	8.5	6.5	26.3	15.3
−15	5.4	2.3	* 8.2	13.2	19.7	11.5	9.3	31.1	18.8
−10	7.8	4.4	* 5.3	16.5	23.6	14.9	12.3	36.4	22.6
−5	10.4	6.7	* 2.0	20.1	27.9	18.5	15.7	42.6	26.7
0	13.3	9.1	* 0.8	24.0	32.6	22.5	19.4	48.2	31.1
5	16.4	12.0	2.7	28.3	37.7	26.9	23.5	54.9	35.9
10	19.7	14.9	4.8	32.8	43.1	31.6	27.9	62.1	41.0
15	23.3	18.1	7.2	37.8	49.0	36.7	32.7	69.9	46.5
20	27.2	21.6	9.7	43.1	55.3	42.3	37.9	78.2	52.5
25	31.4	25.4	12.5	48.8	62.2	48.3	43.5	87.2	58.8
30	36.0	29.4	15.4	54.9	69.3	54.8	49.6	96.8	65.6
35	40.8	33.8	18.7	61.5	77.1	61.8	56.1	107.0	72.8
40	46.0	38.4	22.2	68.5	85.4	69.4	63.2	118.0	80.5
45	51.6	43.4	26.0	76.1	94.2	77.4	70.7	129.5	88.7
50	57.5	48.8	30.0	84.1	104.0	86.1	78.8	142.0	97.4
55	63.8	54.5	34.4	92.6	115.0	114.0	108.0	156.0	106.6
60	70.6	60.6	39.1	101.6	126.0	125.0	118.0	170.0	116.4
65	77.7	67.0	44.1	111.3	137.0	137.0	129.0	185.0	126.7
70	85.3	73.9	49.5	121.4	149.0	149.0	141.0	200.0	137.6
75	93.4	81.3	55.2	132.2	162.0	162.0	153.0	217.0	149.1
80	101.9	89.0	61.3	143.7	175.0	175.0	166.0	235.0	161.2
85	110.9	97.2	67.8	155.7	190.0	190.0	180.0	254.0	174.0
90	120.5	106.0	74.8	168.4	205.0	205.0	194.0	274.0	187.4
95	130.5	115.0	82.1	181.8	220.0	221.0	209.0	295.0	201.4
100	141.1	125.0	89.9	196.0	237.0	238.0	226.0	317.0	216.2
105	152.2	135.0	98.2	210.8	254.0	255.0	242.0	340.0	231.7
110	163.9	146.0	107.0	226.4	273.0	274.0	260.0	364.0	247.9
115	176.3	157.0	116.0	242.8	292.0	293.0	279.0	390.0	264.9
120	189.2	169.0	126.0	260.0	312.0	314.0	299.0	417.0	282.7
125	202.7	182.0	136.0	278.1	333.0	335.0	319.0	445.0	301.3
130	216.9	195.0	147.0	297.0	356.0	358.0	341.0	475.0	320.6
135	231.8	209.0	158.0	316.7	379.0	382.0	363.0	506.0	341.2
140	247.4	223.0	171.0	337.4	404.0	406.0	387.0	538.0	362.6
145	263.7	239.0	183.0	359.1	430.0	432.0	412.0	573.0	384.9
150	280.7	255.0	196.0	381.7	457.0	459.0	438.0	608.0	408.4

Pressures are shown as psig, except (*) indicates inches of mercury vacuum.

Temperature-pressure chart

RSES
The HVACR Training Authority

1911 Rohlwing Road, Suite A   Rolling Meadows, IL 60008   800-297-5660   www.rses.org

RSES
The HVACR Training Authority

Since 1933, RSES' mission has been to enhance technical competence by offering comprehensive, cutting-edge education and certification to its Members and the HVACR industry. The most inclusive and effective way to engage with RSES is to become a Member. Not only will you be joining an advanced group of industry specialists with a wide array of knowledge, but you will also be gaining access to several career-enhancing assets, including (but not limited to):

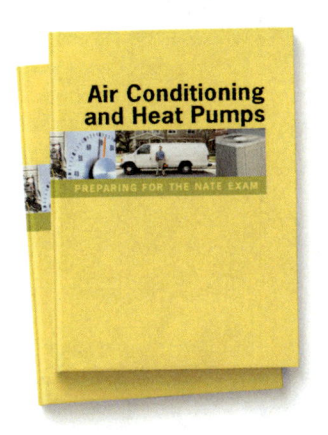

TRAINING—RSES publishes various comprehensive industry training and reference materials and delivers superior educational programs covering all aspects of the HVACR industry. CEUs/CEHs are issued to those who participate in an instructor-led course or complete an RSES eLearning training module or course online.

RSES JOURNAL—*RSES Journal* provides high-quality technical content monthly that can be applied while on the jobsite, as well as interactive columns, new products, news and more. In addition to gaining access to the digital edition, archives dating back to 1995 are also available to Members.

WEBINARS—Webinars feature industry experts presenting on a variety of topics. Each one is presented by some of the industry's most sought-after technical experts. Sessions range from basic to advanced levels on topics spanning the HVACR spectrum. Participation in live webinars earns Members CEUs/CEHs automatically, and all webinars are recorded for future viewing.

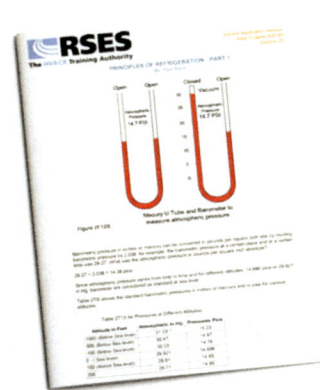

SERVICE APPLICATION MANUAL (SAM)—*SAM* contains literally thousands of pages of technical data, equipment analyses and evaluations, field application instruction, regulations, good practice codes, business development guidance and more. Obtain access to the hundreds of SAM chapters in 25 categories and 45 subcategories of HVACR-related topics.

DISCOUNTS—Member discounts on training and educational opportunities can save you between 10% and 54% on RSES products, online training and more.

JOIN NOW!

Fill out the application on the reverse side and start utilizing these resources today! You can also apply online at www.rses.org.

INDIVIDUAL MEMBERSHIP APPLICATION

RSES 1911 Rohlwing Road, Suite A Rolling Meadows, IL 60008-1397
Phone: 800-297-5660 or 847-297-6464 Fax: 847-297-5038 Web site: www.rses.org

RSES — The HVACR Training Authority

FOR HEADQUARTERS USE ONLY

MC _____ Member No. _____ Chapter No. _____ BC _____

PLEASE TYPE OR PRINT CLEARLY the information you wish to be shown on all RSES records and correspondence. ❑ Mr. ❑ Mrs. ❑ Ms.

First name _____ MI ____ Last name _____

Home address _____ Apt.# _____

City _____ State/Province _____ Zip/Postal Code _____

Country _____ Phone _____ Cell _____

Fax _____ E-mail _____

Month/Day/Year of birth _____

RSES member within the last 3 years? ❑ Yes ❑ No Member No. _____ CM ____ CMS ____

Send mailings to my: ❑ Home address (above) ❑ Business address (below)

Please check if you DO NOT wish to receive: Press releases, notices, announcements, and other information from RSES and the RSES Educational Foundation via: ❑ E-mail ❑ Fax

Business-related third-party offers via: ❑ Direct mail ❑ E-mail ❑ Fax

Having agreed to abide by the Society Bylaws, and those of any Chapter or subsidiary association to which I may belong, I hereby officially apply for membership in RSES.

Signature _____ Date _____

EDUCATION/EMPLOYMENT INFORMATION

School Name (most recent) _____ Years attended _____

City _____ State/Province _____ Area of study _____

Employer Name (current or most recent) _____

Address _____

City _____ State/Province _____ Zip/Postal Code _____

Country _____ Phone _____ Alt. Phone _____

Fax _____ E-mail _____

PAYMENT METHOD

New Member Dues (check one) ❑ One year: $128.00 ❑ Two years: $230.40 (save 10%) ❑ Three years: $326.40 (save 15%)

❑ Check enclosed (make payable to RSES in U.S. dollars)

Credit card ❑ VISA ❑ MASTERCARD ❑ AMERICAN EXPRESS ❑ DISCOVER

Card No. _____ Expiration date _____

Authorized signature _____ CCV _____

Note: A special *RSES Journal* individual subscription price ($18 per year) is included in membership dues. Members may not deduct the subscription price from dues. To determine if RSES membership dues are tax-deductible, consult your tax advisor.

ANSWERS REQUIRED

1. **My primary HVACR role is:** (check one)
   - ❑ Contractor
   - ❑ Service Technician/Installer
   - ❑ Operations/Maintenance Manager/Engineer/Technician
   - ❑ Engineer
   - ❑ Sales
   - ❑ Instructor
   - ❑ Student
   - ❑ Other _____ (please specify)

2. **My firm's business is:** (check one)
   - ❑ Contractor: 1–3 technicians
   - ❑ Contractor: 4–10 technicians
   - ❑ Contractor: 11–19 technicians
   - ❑ Contractor: 20+ technicians
   - ❑ HVACR industry OEM
   - ❑ Industrial (manufacturing or processing, not HVACR industry)
   - ❑ Wholesaler/Distributor
   - ❑ Commercial/Institutional/Government Agency/Association
   - ❑ Other _____ (please specify)

3. **I heard about RSES from:** (check one)
   - ❑ Seminar
   - ❑ Chapter
   - ❑ Friend
   - ❑ Employer
   - ❑ School/Instructor
   - ❑ Member (current/former)
   - ❑ Direct mail
   - ❑ Internet
   - ❑ *RSES Journal*
   - ✓ Other EORD16 (please specify)

4. **My e-mail preferences:** (check all that apply)
   - ❑ Conference
   - ❑ Seminars
   - ❑ Regional/Association/Chapter news
   - ❑ General news
   - ❑ Training and testing news
   - ❑ Product news
   - ❑ Chapter Officer news
   - ❑ *RSES Journal* updates
   - ❑ *RSES Journal* news and Web exclusives
   - ❑ *RSES Journal* e-newsletters
   - ❑ Industry news and events
   - ❑ Membership benefits
   - ❑ Business-related third-party offers